fabulous fabric beads

fabulous fabric

beads

CREATE CUSTOM BEADS *and* ART JEWELRY

kristal *wick*

INTERWEAVE.
interweavebooks.com

Editor ANNE MERROW
Art Direction/Design CONNIE POOLE
Photography JOE COCA
Step-by-step Photography ANN SWANSON
Photo Styling ANN SWANSON
Technical Editor JAMIE HOGSETT

Interweave Press LLC
201 East Fourth Street
Loveland, CO 80537-5655 USA
interweavebooks.com

Printed in China through Asia Pacific Offset.

Library of Congress Cataloging-in-Publication Data

Wick, Kristal
  Fabulous fabric beads : create custom beads and art jewelry / Kristal Wick,
author.
      p. cm.
  Includes bibliographical references and index.
  ISBN 978-1-59668-077-7 (pbk.)
  1. Jewelry making. 2. Beads. 3. Textile crafts. I. Title.
  TT212.W5 2008
  745.594'2--dc22

                                        2008008685

10 9 8 7 6 5 4 3 2 1

This book is dedicated to all those creative souls who ignore the discouraging voices and take the brave dive into the depths of discovering their creative hearts and fearlessly let go!

Thanks to...

The great gang at Interweave. Friends—without my supportive tribe, this project wouldn't be nearly as inspired and I wouldn't have even an ounce of sanity left! Starbucks, for supplying me with the nectar of the Gods: eggnog lattes. My students. My muses, Sage and Gaia, whose unconditional love and hilarious comic relief are the truest "bling" in my life. Katie Hacker, Karen Carruthers, Marlene Blessing, Sherrill Kahn, Laura Murray, Jan and John Gray, my family, and especially James Plagmann, whose endless support is deeply appreciated! Special thanks to Dave the cat for loving companionship and stimulating conversation when needed the most.

To the many manufacturers who have so generously donated materials for this book: Absolute Crystal Components, Alacarte Clasps; AMACO, Beadalon; The Bead Goes On; Clear Snap; Fusion Beads; Gita Maria; Grafix Arts; Green Girl Studios, Ilene Combs Blanco Inc.; Jacquard; Laura Murray Designs; Lillypilly Designs; Lucky Squirrel; Paula Radke; Plaid; Ranger; Shrinky Dinks; Somerset Silver; Swarovski, Tierra Cast; Two Cranes, Vintaj; and Weldbond.

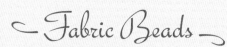

~ Fabric Beads ~

Foreword

From the first moment I opened *Fabulous Fabric Beads*, I was overwhelmed by pages filled with gorgeous color—it's like holding your favorite sundae in your hands and savoring each bite. Kristal Wick's enthusiasm leaps out from every artistic and inviting page, and I was instantly eager to try every technique and project.

I am fortunate to have Kristal as my friend, and in person she is always happy and eager to share her vast knowledge. Her color sense is amazing and she is constantly experimenting with new ideas. In the pages of this book, she shares that enthusiasm with you. With clear images and directions, the easy techniques and superb projects come to life. Everything from basic supplies to detailed directions for making finished beads into jewelry is shown in beautiful close-up photographs, beautifully and concisely explained.

Whether you are an experienced jewelry artist or these ideas are all new to you, *Fabulous Fabric Beads* is full of "aha!" moments—even though I use some of these surface design techniques, I found myself saying, "I wish I had thought of that!" on almost every page. I can't wait to try some of the techniques since so many are new to me, like foiling (page 40), using grids (page 27), using gesso on fabric (page 35), and bleaching (page 34). After you've made beads to your heart's content,

Kristal's jewelry-making projects and gallery of jewelry ideas open up all sorts of possibilities. I can't wait to make Wire Whimsy (page 80), the Delicado Bracelet (page 82), and especially the Wild Fiber Necklace (page 98). The glossary of stringing techniques is especially helpful for a novice like me.

This book is a true winner—full of imaginative and original techniques.

Sherrill Kahn

9

Welcome

I am so excited to share my fabric bead secrets with you! After years of making dichroic glass jewelry, I heard my customers ask for something lighter—their earlobes were dangling too low after years of "earlobe abuse." So I set out on a journey to capture the vibrant colors of dichroic glass with some kind of weightless material that was durable and exciting. Thus Sassy Silkies, my original handpainted silk scrolls, were born. They were my first fabric bead babies, and since then they have been joined in my repertoire with lots of fun new beads!

While you're exploring the projects and techniques in this book, have no fear of making mistakes when it comes to creating your own fabric beads. Many times a "mistake" has turned out to be hugely successful in ways I'd never imagined or showed me a better way to do something. Plop that paintbrush on that silk and go with the flow! Always remember there's plenty of fabric available, so experiment all you want. Go outside the box and break the rules! I believe that when it comes to true art there aren't any rules, just a whisper inside directing you to add a dab of this or that color and see what happens. You can always add another layer or paint over it!

So many of us have stashes of our favorite fabrics, beads, buttons, and other materials. Fabulous Fabric Beads are a great way to use your stash and scraps, since you need so little fabric to create these beauties.

What's important is to embrace the creative process and PLAY! My hope for this book is to act as your tour guide and provide endless inspiration along your creative path. Now, take a deep breath and go make cool stuff!

Kristal

materials & tools

There are tons of fun supplies on the market for making and decorating beads. These are some of my favorites. Most of the materials can be found at your local craft, bead, quilting, or fabric stores.

Fabrics

You can use all types of fabric for making beads. Smoother fabrics work better, but some nubby fabrics can result in rich textured treasures, so feel free to play. I've had the most luck with silks and cottons. There's no need to prewash your fabric, just use it as is. If you're not sure how a technique will turn out, practice on a small swatch first.

Always trim your fabrics after you paint and embellish them. The scraps are wonderful to use in other projects.

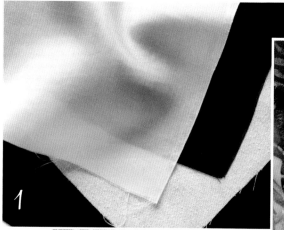

1. Silks
Silk is my favorite fabric for beads. There are many different types of silks, but my top two picks are China silk for its sheer, light quality and douppioni silk for its lovely stiff body. Douppioni silk behaves like stiff paper when you're sewing, gluing, or rolling because the body of the fabric is quite stiff.

2. Cotton
There's a wide variety of designs and weights of commercial cotton, and you can embellish the surface of all of them. When making beads out of cotton, either use the adhesive method or cut really long lengths of fabrics to add enough body to your bead (see page 48).

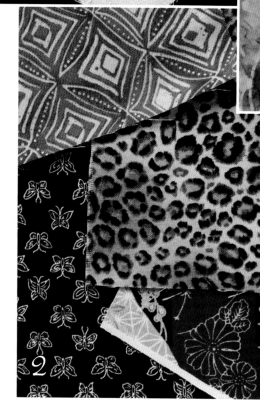

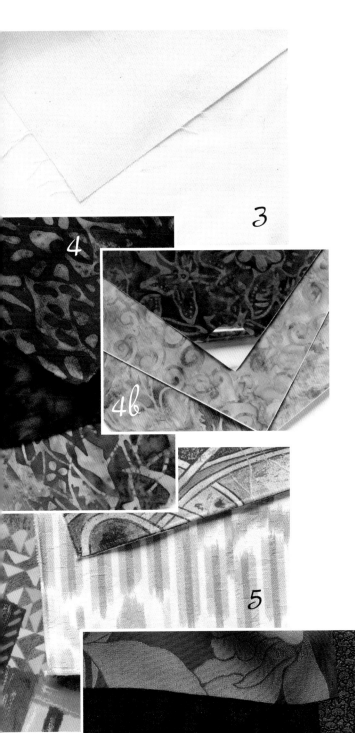

3. Muslin

Muslin is blank cotton—it's fun to paint and dye. The result is often more textured than silk due to the bumps in the fabric. I think muslin gives a more ethnic flavor to the bead, while silk is more elegant.

4. Batiks

Batiks are richly dyed cottons that are great to embellish and use for beads. I use regular batik fabrics as well as batiks with an adhesive backing (see 4b) that are specially designed for crafting.

5. Recycled

Recycled fabrics can mean many different things these days, but my personal favorites are from my local interior design center. They're usually more than happy to give you old fabric samples. These samples tend to be stiff designer fabrics that are perfect for making fabric beads. You can also check thrift stores, garage sales, and flea markets for old placemats and clothing that will work well for making fabric beads.

6. Vintage kimono fabric

You can sometimes find very small precious pieces of authentic vintage kimono fabric, perfect for making fabric beads. Quite often these fabrics are stained or faded; just embellish with paint, Paintstiks, or foils to cover up the flaws. I love to reflect on the journey this simple piece of cloth must have made before ending up in my hands. It's fun to ponder the possibilities of this special fabric while you're creating.

Glue and epoxy

Basic Bead Supplies

You'll need most of these tools and materials to make basic fabric beads—they're the staples in the fabric beadmaker's studio.

Acrylic sealers
Use a spray sealer for anything you print on the computer. The ink is just sitting on the top of the surface and doesn't sink in, so once the ink is dry you need to seal it. If you want your fabric bead nice and hard, apply a thin coat of Mod Podge to the completed bead and let dry.

Adhesives
It's good to know which particular adhesive to use for a specific process; I'll give you my recommendations for each project. The main adhesives we'll use in this book are 2-part epoxy, Weldbond, fabric glue, and Mod Podge.

Adhesive-backed paper
Use these sheets to adhere to the back side of your fabric instead of fabric glue to roll them into beads.

Freezer paper
Iron freezer paper onto the back of fabrics to run through your printer.

Iron
Cotton and silk are both prone to wrinkling, and for polished fabric beads, you'll need smooth fabric. Keep an iron handy for quick touch-ups.

Acrylic sealer and
Mod Podge adhesive

Rotary cutter, ruler, iron,
and self-healing cutting mat

Rolling rods

One of the keys to making great fabric beads are the rolling rods. Collect different sizes and play with the results. My favorites are plastic straws, steel dowels, and double-pointed knitting needles.

Rotary cutter

Rotary cutters really speed up your cutting process. Be careful, those blades are sharp!

Ruler

I use a clear quilting ruler with a lip on one edge, so I can quickly move it on the cutting mat to make straight cuts of fabric.

Scissors

You'll use fabric scissors to cut your fabrics. You'll also need some other sharp scissors to cut your painted fabrics. It's also fun to use decorative scissors for the copper beads (see page 62).

Self-healing cutting mat

This is an invaluable tool for making fabric beads. Cutting mats come in many sizes, so use the one that feels comfortable to you and your work space.

Spatula

Use a rubber or silicone spatula to spread glue evenly.

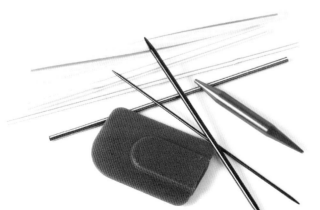

Rolling rods
and spatula

materials & tools

Surface Design & Embellishment

Crystals and seed beads

Don't limit yourself to products in the fabric aisle—using all kinds of decorations can make your fabric beads totally unique!

Battery-operated toothbrush

These are great for splattering techniques and cleaning rubber stamps. (Thanks to Sherrill Kahn for the idea!)

Beads

Seed beads come in many sizes, shapes, and colors. I use them in everything! There are all kinds of other artisan beads that are fun to incorporate into your creations. Use them as a focal piece or as filler beads accenting your fabric bead jewelry.

Bleach

I had to try a bleach pen on my fabric beads! Yes, they work on cotton fabrics and dyed fabrics; I especially like them on black cotton. They will not work on acrylic painted fabrics.

Copper sheets

Copper can be stamped, texturized, and cut to apply to beads. Use an embossing gun to treat copper sheets once they're stamped.

Crystals

Swarovski rules! I could go on and on about how this pretty sparkly embellishment has brightened up my life. Come to the "light" side and play with these favorite shiny jewels! In addition to traditional rounds and bicones, crystals are now available as stars, hearts, squares . . . almost any shape you can imagine. I also use a wide variety of Swarovski flatback crystals, which are available in many colors and sizes. It's fun to pull together a color scheme by matching crystal beads and flatbacks in a finished project.

Tiny beads and crystal flatbacks

Spray dye and Tee
Juice markers

Embossing gun and
copper sheets

Dyes

There are many ways to dye your fabrics! Three of my unconventional favorites are spray dyes, good old coffee, and Tee Juice markers. Designed to mark on T-shirts, Tee Juice markers can be used to apply dye easily and precisely to almost any fabric.

Embossing gun

Use an embossing gun with embossing powders, or if you're in a hurry and want to dry fabric quickly. Be careful, as acrylic paint can bubble if it gets too hot.

Embossing powders

These powders puff up when you heat them with an embossing gun. They come in a huge variety of colors and textures, from fine to very thick. You can apply them with a rubber stamp using pigment ink or hand draw using a pigment ink pen.

Fibers

Available as fusible film and shredded fiber, sparkly Angelina is such a fun product to play with. You'll find so many creative ways to use this synthetic material. The Angelina beads on page 67 are just a first step—take it further and experiment!

Foils

One of my favorite embellishing techniques is foiling on fabrics. Using an iron, you can foil on commercial fabrics, custom silks, almost anything.

Hole punches and die cuts

Hole punches come in many different sizes and shapes. You can get really creative with these!

Foils and adhesive

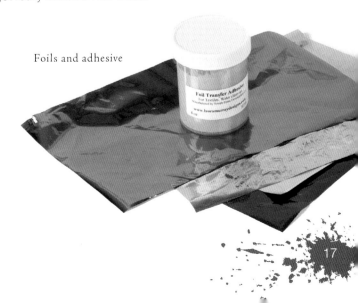

Embossing pad and
powders

17

Ink, ink pad, and
stamp cleaner

Inks

Use ink pads or apply inks directly from the bottles on a sponge. Clearsnap makes blank ink pads to create your own ink pad by adding ink or paint.

Ink pads

Most of the ink pads I use are permanent inks and require their own special ink cleaner. My favorite permanent ink pads are Staz On fast-drying solvent ink.

Metallic markers

These are fun for embellishing many things, particularly the edges of wooden beads.

Paints

Paints can be overwhelming, as there are so many types of paints on the market. I use mainly Folk Art acrylic paints for my fabric base coat. They give the fabric a layer of stiffness that makes it easier to work with and more durable. Then I like to embellish with Jacquard paints. I love the colors and depth of Jacquard. (When preparing your fabric, keep this in mind that these do not dry stiff.) I often apply a base coat of Folk Art, then embellish top layers with Jacquard. Neopaque and Sherrill's Sorbets are opaque, so they cover quite well. I also love Lumiere paints, especially metallics. Shiva Oil Paintstiks are great to use alone or in layering with other techniques. Paintstiks are oil-based paint in stick form, so make sure you protect your work surface and wear old clothes. They can be messy!

Paint brushes,
Paintstiks, and paints

Natural and synthetic
sponges

Paint brushes

I use a variety of brushes: small fine brushes for embellishing and lots of foam brushes for painting large fabric surfaces. Stencil brushes are also handy for stenciling.

Rubber stamps

Some of my favorite rubber stamps are in Sherrill Kahn's Impress Me line, which are unmounted and easy to clean. Really detailed stamps can be tricky on fabric, so experiment on scrap fabrics first if you're uncertain whether the stamp has too much detail.

Rubbing templates and texture pads

These are generally unmounted and come in handy when doing most any kind of fabric painting. They work well with Paintstiks and foiling. I also use them as stamps. You can use masking tape to mask off a small portion of the template.

Salt

Salting is a technique used in painting that works well for fabric, too (see page 30). There are many different types and sizes of salt. I like larger rock salt or sea salt, but any type will work.

Sponges

These come in all shapes and sizes. I like using the natural sea sponges best, as they have very random and textured patterns. You can also cut out your own shapes using compressed cellulose sponges that expand in water. Before expanding, the sponge lays flat, making it easy to draw or stencil a shape before wetting the sponge. They can also be torn or cut with scissors or a knife.

Stencils, rubbing templates,
and stamps

Stencils

You can purchase these or make your own. For fabric beads, I use stencils with really small designs and very few details, as only a small area of the fabric bead shows after you roll it.

Teflon sheet

Use this thin flexible sheet to protect your work surface from the heat of an embossing gun.

Stringing tools

Once you've made some amazing fabric beads, how can you turn them into jewelry? There are lots of jewelry findings available, but these are the bare necessities.

Beading wire

Beading wire comes in fun colors and different strengths. For wire wrapping, I use Artistic Wire, which is stiffer than wire for stringing.

Beading tools

The most commonly used tools for the stringing projects in this book are wire cutters, chain-nose pliers, round-nose pliers, and flat-nose pliers.

Beading wire

Chain-nose pliers, flat-nose pliers, round-nose pliers, and wire cutters

There are oodles of surface design techniques you can apply to fabric. I've described some of my favorites, but I encourage you to push the boundaries and create your own favorites.

Surface Design Techniques

From a little bit of paint from the craft store to elaborate techniques with specialty tools and products, there are so many ways of changing the look of ordinary fabric. Dress it up or down, add or subtract color, build layers of effects—use the ideas here to create your own dazzling cloth that will make your fabric beads one of a kind.

Painting
Painting fabrics can open new doors for all kinds of projects. I often find a great fabric that's missing some pizzazz or a splash of a particular color. Painting fabric is a quick way to customize your designs and create unique beads.

ACRYLIC BASE COAT
There are many different kinds of acrylic paints. The kinds I use mainly come in bottles and jars. I apply a base color of liquid acrylic from a bottle (usually metallic Folk Art), then embellish with Jacquard jar paints such as Lumiere or Sherrill's Sorbets.

Note
Always remember to trim your fabrics **after** you paint and embellish them. The scraps are wonderful to use in other projects.

Heat-setting Fabrics

Some dyes and paints need to be heat-set with an iron. It's a good idea to get into the habit of ironing the back of all fabrics. It sets the paints permanently and also gets the wrinkles out. Once the fabric is completely dry, lay it face down on an ironing board or on a flexible Teflon sheet. Iron the fabric on the appropriate setting.

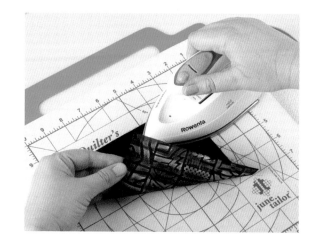

Supplies

- ✕ Acrylic paints
- ✕ Fabric
- ✕ Foam brush
- ✕ Spray bottle filled with water
- ✕ Newspapers or newsprint
- ✕ Iron and ironing board

1. Prepare the paint by making sure it's the consistency of skim milk. If the paint is too thick, add water to the paint bottle and shake well.

2. Lay fabric on top of 3–4 sheets of newspaper or newsprint.

3. Spray fabric with water (Figure 1). Saturate the foam brush with water as well.

4. Squirt some paint onto the fabric (Figure 2) and spread it evenly with the brush (Figure 3).

5. Continue adding paint and spraying water onto fabric if needed (Figure 4).

6. Place fabric on another clean sheet of newspaper or newsprint or hang to dry. (If you leave your wet fabric to dry on the same newspaper you painted on, the paper will stick to the back of the fabric and you'll have a mess to clean up!)

7. Once fabric is dry, iron the back side of the fabric on the appropriate setting.

Now you are ready to layer spectacular designs on your fabric!

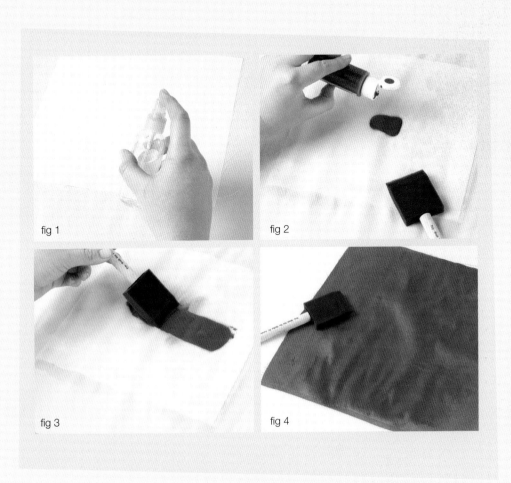

fig 1

fig 2

fig 3

fig 4

SPONGING

This is my favorite technique for creating a layered, mottled effect. It's easy and highly addictive! I like to layer two or three colors, but sometimes I've used five or six different colors on one fabric. Starting with three colors you like usually results in pleasing effects.

Some great color combinations:
Elegant: Gold, silver, and bronze on a dark base color such as black or teal
Subtle: Taupe and gold on a beige base
Daring: Orange, gold, and bronze on a red base

Supplies

- ✕ Paints
- ✕ Fabric
- ✕ Sponge
- ✕ Disposable plate
- ✕ Spray bottle filled with water
- ✕ Newspapers or newsprint
- ✕ Iron and ironing board

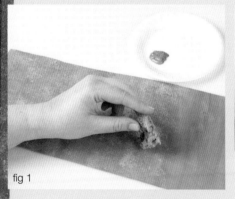

fig 1

fig 2

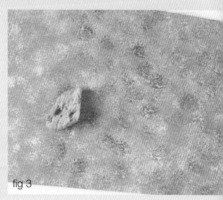

fig 3

1. If desired, paint the base fabric (see page 24).

2. Soak sponge in water and wring out; the sponge should be damp, not dripping wet.

3. Pour a dollop of paint onto the plate. Dab the sponge in the paint, then dab a few times on the plate so the sponge isn't overloaded.

4. Dab the sponge onto fabric randomly, being sure to turn the sponge around each time so you get a varied texture, not the same shape each time. Blending your sponge placements is key to fabulous texturing **(Figure 1)**. Reload the sponge with more paint and repeat until you have achieved the desired effect.

5. Repeat Steps 3 and 4 with more paint colors as desired **(Figures 2 and 3)**. Allow the fabric to dry.

6. Iron the back of the dry fabric on the appropriate setting.

Note

It's fun to make your own sponges using Miracle Sponges, which can be found at finer cooking supply stores or online. Draw any shape onto a Miracle Sponge and cut it out. Wet the sponge and stamp.

GRIDS

The hardware store is filled with a wide variety of grids used for fences. I like the smaller grids that can be cut with heavy-duty wire cutters. Don't use your good beading wire cutter for cutting the grids.

Supplies

- ✖ Paints
- ✖ Fabric
- ✖ Sponge
- ✖ Metal file
- ✖ Wire grid
- ✖ Wire snippers
- ✖ Disposable plate
- ✖ Newspapers or newsprint
- ✖ Iron and ironing board

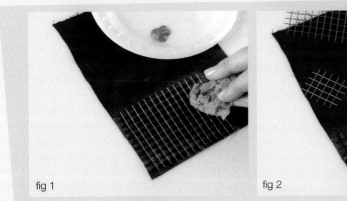

fig 1

fig 2

1. Cut out a section of wire grid. Be very careful, as the edges are sharp.

2. Smooth the edges with a file.

3. Soak sponge in water and wring out; the sponge should be damp, not dripping wet.

4. Pour a dollop of paint onto the plate. Dab the sponge in the paint, then dab a few times on the plate so the sponge isn't overloaded.

5. Place grid on fabric. Daub paint on top of the grid (**Figure 1**). Reload the sponge with more paint and repeat until you have achieved the desired effect (**Figure 2**).

6. Repeat Steps 4 and 5 with additional colors if desired.

7. Iron the back of the dry fabric on the appropriate setting.

STENCILING

Stencils with simpler, less detailed designs work best on fabric.

Supplies

✘ Paints
✘ Fabric
✘ Stencils
✘ Stencil brush or dauber
✘ Disposable plate
✘ Newspapers or newsprint
✘ Masking tape (optional)
✘ Iron and ironing board

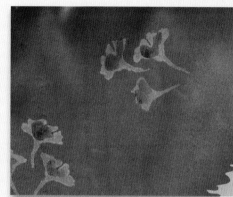

Note

Make your own stencils by using a stencil cutter to cut a design out of clear acetate.

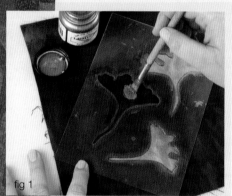

fig 1

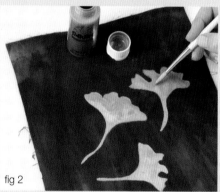

fig 2

fig 3

1. Place stencil on fabric. (If desired, secure the stencil on the fabric with masking tape.)

2. Be sure that the paint is the right consistency: It should be fairly thick, like heavy cream. If it's too thin, the paint will run under the stencil; if it's too thick, the paint will glob up your stencil. Dip a stiff stencil brush or dauber into paint and dab off the excess paint. Using a swirling motion, apply the paint inside the stencil (**Figure 1**). Reload the brush with paint as needed. If you want to place the stencil down again on your fabric, make sure you clean it between placements to avoid smudging.

3. Remove stencil and let the paint dry.

4. Once paint is dry add an accent color in the middle of the stenciled design (**Figure 2**). Let dry.

5. Add a third accent color in the middle of the design (**Figure 3**). Let dry.

6. Iron the back of the dry fabric on the appropriate setting.

SCRUNCHING

This technique works best on blank white silk using metallic paints. It's a bit messy, so gather all your materials ahead of time and wear gloves.

Supplies

- ✖ Metallic acrylic paints
- ✖ Fabric
- ✖ Rubber gloves
- ✖ Foam brush
- ✖ Spray bottle filled with water
- ✖ Newspapers or newsprint
- ✖ Iron and ironing board

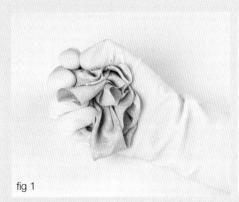

fig 1

fig 2

1. Follow Steps 1–5 of the basic method for painting fabric (see page 24).

2. While the silk is still wet, wad it up into a ball starting from the middle of the silk (Figure 1).

3. Carefully unfold the fabric and re-wad two or three times; with each "scrunch," you add more texture (Figure 2). Leave the silk wadded up and let dry on a fresh piece of newspaper.

4. Iron the back of the dry fabric on the appropriate setting.

creating surface designs on fabric

SALTING

This technique is fun, easy, and great to do with kids. Salt comes in different size granules; larger chunks such as rock salt create large spots, while fine salt creates smaller spots. Experiment until you find your favorite salt.

Supplies

- ✘ Acrylic paints
- ✘ Fabric
- ✘ Salt
- ✘ Rubber gloves
- ✘ Plastic sheet
- ✘ Foam brush
- ✘ Spray bottle filled with water
- ✘ Newspapers or newsprint
- ✘ Iron and ironing board

1. Place the fabric on a sheet of plastic. (Unlike other techniques where the water is absorbed into the newspaper, the success of the salting technique depends on the water sitting in small puddles.)

2. Follow Steps 1–5 of the basic method for painting fabric (see page 24) (Figure 1).

3. While the fabric is still wet, sprinkle salt on the surface (Figure 2).

4. Spray just a bit of water on the fabric, being careful not to drench it. Leave the fabric lying flat to dry completely.

5. Brush salt off the dried fabric (Figures 3 and 4).

6. Iron the back side of the fabric on the appropriate setting.

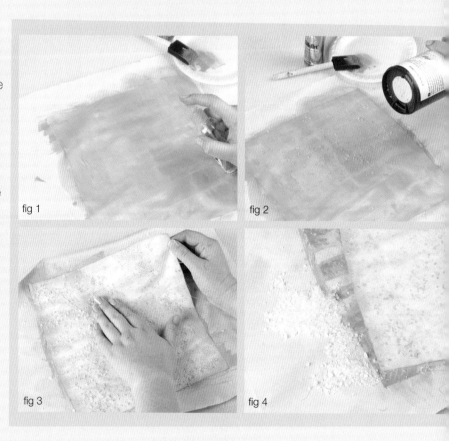

fig 1

fig 2

fig 3

fig 4

SPLATTERING

You can splatter a variety of colors onto fabric or splatter on top of painted fabric to add another layer of texture. You'll want to wear gloves for this project and do it outside if possible.

Supplies

- ✗ Paints
- ✗ Fabric
- ✗ Rubber gloves
- ✗ Foam brush
- ✗ Disposable plate
- ✗ Toothbrush
- ✗ Spray bottle filled with water
- ✗ Newspapers or newsprint
- ✗ Iron and ironing board

Note
Try an electric toothbrush and splatter away!

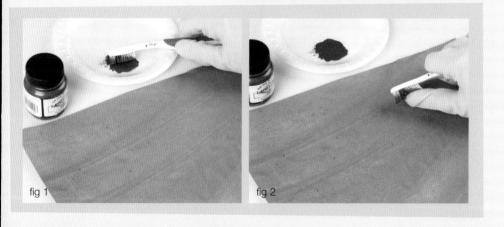

fig 1   fig 2

1. Lay a piece of prepared fabric on newspaper.
2. Squeeze out a dollop of paint onto the plate. (For this technique, thicker paint works better.)
3. Dip the toothbrush into paint (**Figure 1**).
4. Run your thumb through the brush bristles, splattering the fabric with paint (**Figure 2**). Repeat until the desired effect is achieved.
5. Allow paint to dry completely.
6. Iron the back of the dry fabric on the appropriate setting.

Dyeing

Two of my favorite techniques are spray dyeing and Tee Juice markers. I have fallen in love with Ranger's Adirondack Color Wash sprays. This is the quickest method of dyeing fabric—perfect for immediate gratification gals like me! I like to use two to four complementary colors for this technique. The Tee Juice markers allow you to draw directly on the fabric, giving the permanence of dye and the control of a marker. And look no further for a lovely dye than your own pantry: Yummy coffee dyeing gives you a soft, subtly earthy effect without that caffeine jolt!

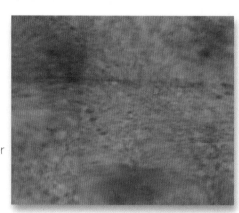

SPRAY DYEING

Supplies

* ✖ Spray dyes
* ✖ Fabric
* ✖ Spray bottle filled with water
* ✖ Newspapers or newsprint
* ✖ Iron and ironing board

fig 1   fig 2

1. Place the fabric on 3–4 sheets of newspaper or newsprint.

2. Spray fabric with water.

3. Holding bottle back far enough so there is an even stream, spray first color on fabric (**Figure 1**). (Holding the bottle close to the fabric can make the dye clumpy or splotchy. If you like, experiment with that effect.) For more intense colors, skip Step 2 and spray dyes directly on dry fabric.

4. Repeat Step 3 with other colors as desired (**Figure 2**), keeping in mind that using too many colors can make the fabric look muddy. Allow the fabric to dry completely.

5. Iron the back of the dry fabric on the appropriate setting.

Note

Be sure to check out the back side of the fabric. It can be just as interesting as the front. Feel free to use the other side.

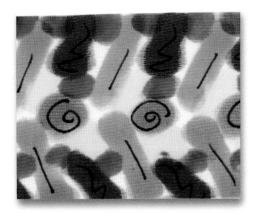

TEE JUICE MARKER DYEING

Supplies

- ✗ Tee Juice fabric markers
- ✗ White cotton or silk
- ✗ Iron and ironing board

Note
I create a lot of my designs with simple abstract lines and circles—no fancy drawing skills necessary.

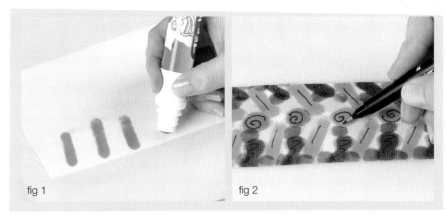

fig 1   fig 2

1. Draw on the fabric with fat markers (Figure 1).
2. Add details with the thin markers (Figure 2).
3. Iron the back of the dry fabric on the appropriate setting.

COFFEE DYEING

Supplies

- ✗ Strong coffee or espresso
- ✗ Fabric
- ✗ Newspapers or newsprint
- ✗ Iron and ironing board

fig 1   fig 2

1. Place the fabric in a cup filled with coffee (Figure 1). Allow to soak overnight (Figure 2).
2. Wring out the fabric (do not rinse) Allow it to dry.
3. Iron the back of the dry fabric on the appropriate setting.

Bleaching

I love beach pens for hand-drawing directly on fabric. This process works well directly on dark fabrics. It will not work on fabric that has been painted with acrylics.

Supplies

* Fabric
* Bleach pen
* Baking soda
* Iron and ironing board

fig 1

fig 2

1. Make a neutralizer by dissolving a spoonful of baking soda in a cup of warm water.

2. Draw designs onto fabric with bleach pen (Figure 1).

3. Let sit for a minute and rinse with cool water, then quickly dip into neutralizing solution for a few minutes.

4. Rinse again with cool water and let dry (Figure 2).

5. Iron the back of the dry fabric on the appropriate setting.

Note

You can also use bleach pens with rubber stamps by sponging the bleach onto the stamp and pressing onto the fabric.

Gesso

Gesso is normally used by canvas artists as a primer, so look for this product in the canvas painting section of the store. It gives fabric a rough surface and body. This technique works best on dark fabrics.

Supplies

- ✘ Fabric
- ✘ Gesso
- ✘ Disposable plate
- ✘ Texture tools
- ✘ Sponge brush

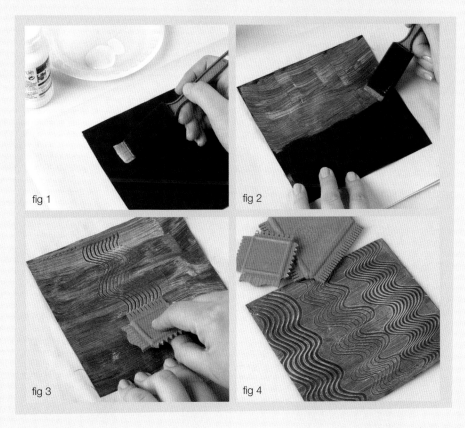

fig 1

fig 2

fig 3

fig 4

1. Pour a dollop of gesso onto the plate.

2. Paint a medium layer of gesso onto your fabric (**Figures 1 and 2**).

3. Using a texture tool, make squiggly lines and shapes in the wet gesso (**Figure 3**).

4. Allow fabric to dry (**Figure 4**). (Do not iron.)

Stamping

I enjoy stamping on fabric with both ink pads and paints. If you are using paints, pay attention to the consistency: If the paint is too thin, it will run and ruin your design. If it's too thick, it will clog up your stamp and leave globs everywhere. With a bit of practice you'll learn to create the right cream-like consistency. Use stamps with basic shapes and simple designs.

STAMPING WITH PAINTS

Supplies

- ✘ Paints
- ✘ Fabric
- ✘ Foam brush
- ✘ Rubber stamps or texture plates
- ✘ Disposable plate

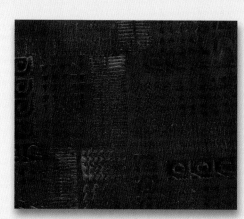

Note

Clean your stamps immediately or soak them in water until you're ready to clean them thoroughly. Soap, water, and a toothbrush will do the trick.

fig 1

fig 2

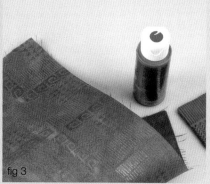

fig 3

1. Pour a dollop of paint onto the plate.
2. Brush a thin layer of paint onto the stamp surface (Figure 1).
3. Place the stamp on the fabric. Press hard without rocking the stamp and lift up (Figure 2).
4. Repeat Steps 2 and 3 as desired (Figure 3).
5. Iron the back of the dry fabric on the appropriate setting.

variation

STAMPING WITH INK PADS Use the same process with a permanent ink pad instead of paint. Be sure to load a lot of ink onto your stamp. You want it to be juicy, not too dry. Clean your stamps immediately after use with the appropriate manufacturer's ink remover.

CARVING CUSTOM STAMPS

Make your own stamps from erasers, which come in a variety of shapes and sizes. You can carve a variety of small erasers, then use them individually or glue them to a block of wood to make one large stamp. When it's finished, use the eraser as you would any other stamp.

Supplies

- ✗ Rubber erasers
- ✗ Pen or pencil
- ✗ Carving tools

1. With the pencil or pen, draw a simple design on the eraser—the less detailed the better (Figure 1).

2. Use a carving tool to slowly and carefully carve away small pieces of the eraser that are not part of your design (Figures 2 and 3).

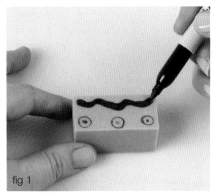
fig 1

fig 2

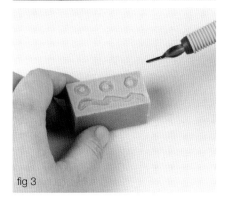
fig 3

Paintstiks

Paintstiks are loads of fun! They are basically oil paints in a stick form and work beautifully on fabrics. You can produce so many different effects by using them alone or in combination with other techniques. You can color directly onto the fabric for a very intense effect or use them with a stencil and stencil brush to get a softer, more airbrushed look. This can be a messy process, so be sure to cover your work surface and wear old clothes or an apron. This paint is permanent.

STENCILING METHOD

Supplies

✘ Paintstiks
✘ Fabric
✘ Paper towels
✘ Stencils
✘ Stencil brush
✘ Iron and ironing board
✘ Blank paper

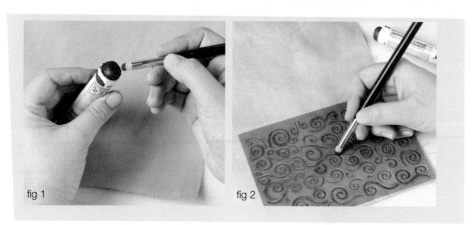

fig 1

fig 2

1. Remove the invisible protective skin coating the outside of the Paintstiks by rubbing the Paintstik on a paper towel until the skin is rubbed off.

2. Load stencil brush with paint from Paintstik by rubbing the brush on the Paintstiks and getting the paint onto the brush (Figure 1).

3. Place stencil on top of fabric. Using a rotating motion, swirl brush inside stencil (Figure 2).

4. Let fabric cure for 3–5 days.

5. Iron the back of the fabric for 10–15 seconds in each area to set the paints.

RUBBING METHOD

Supplies

- ✗ Paintstiks
- ✗ Fabric
- ✗ Paper towels
- ✗ Texture template or stamps
- ✗ Iron and ironing board
- ✗ Blank paper

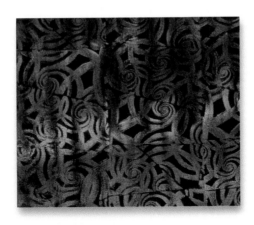

1. Remove the invisible protective skin coating the outside of the Paintstiks by rubbing the Paintstik on a paper towel until the skin is rubbed off.

2. Place fabric on top of texture plate (Figure 1).

3. Rub the Paintstik carefully on the fabric as though coloring with giant crayons. Stroke the fabric with the Paintstik in one direction (Figure 2).

4. The key to achieving great depth of textures is to layer different colors on the fabric. Without moving the fabric, add another color, blending it with the first color (Figure 3).

5. Repeat Step 4 to add a third color.

6. Let the painted fabric dry and cure for 3–5 days.

7. Iron the back of the fabric for 10–15 seconds in each area to set the paints (Figure 4).

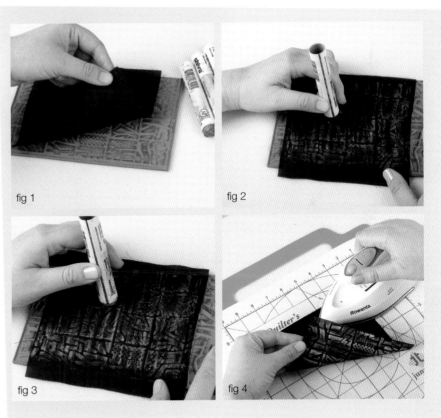

fig 1

fig 2

fig 3

fig 4

Foiling

Plan to have lots of time for this project—stopping is very nearly impossible! My life hasn't been the same since textile artist Laura Murray taught me to foil.

Supplies

- ✘ Foil adhesive
- ✘ Stamps or texture plates
- ✘ Foils
- ✘ Fabric
- ✘ Sponge brush
- ✘ Iron and ironing board

1. Brush foil adhesive onto a stamp or texture plate (**Figure 1**).

2. Place the stamp on the fabric. Press hard without rocking the stamp and lift up (**Figure 2**). Repeat as desired.

3. Allow the foil adhesive to dry. I usually leave it overnight just to be sure.

4. Place a foil sheet on top of the dry adhesive with the colored side up (**Figure 3**).

5. Using a dry iron on the highest setting, burnish the foil by rubbing onto the adhesive with the tip of the iron. (For best results, imagine that you are scraping the foil onto the fabric using the iron.) Rub 3–4 times over the same spot to transfer completely. If the foil starts to flake, turn down the iron.

6. Peel the foil off the adhesive.

7. Repeat Steps 4–6 to cover the rest of the adhesive (**Figure 4**).

fig 1

fig 2

fig 3

fig 4

Computer printing

The sky is truly the limit when it comes to using your computer to decorate fabrics! Scan in designs or draw your own from scratch. There are enough different ways of using the computer to print on fabrics to fill up a whole book, so experiment until you find your favorite way. This very simple method is the one I use often.

Supplies

- ✖ Painted fabric (see page 24), cut to printer size
- ✖ Freezer paper
- ✖ Computer and ink-jet printer
- ✖ Clear acrylic sealer
- ✖ Scissors
- ✖ Iron and ironing board

Note
This process works best when using flat paints on your fabric. Metallic paints don't work as well.

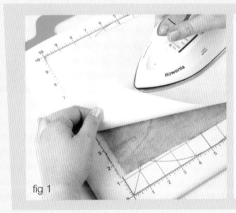

fig 1

fig 2

1. Create a design on your computer or use a picture you have scanned in.

2. Iron the back of the fabric on the appropriate setting so it's very smooth and wrinkle free.

3. Cut a sheet of freezer paper to the same size as the painted fabric. Place it shiny side down on the back of the fabric and iron (**Figure 1**).

4. Run your fabric through your printer, being sure to use the highest-quality setting.

5. Let ink dry and peel off freezer paper.

6. Spray with clear acrylic sealer so ink won't smudge (**Figure 2**).

Combining techniques

Once you've experimented with these surface techniques, combine them to create one-of-a-kind masterpieces! If a piece of fabric doesn't turn out the way I expect, I often combine techniques and go for a completely different effect. For example, if a piece of dyed fabric turns out too muddy, it may be a jewel once you sponge or foil it.

Here are some fabrics that I've embellished in several ways:

1. Stamped, grid stenciled, foiled.
2. Bleached, foiled.
3. Scrunched, stamped.
4. Stamped, Paintstiked, stenciled, foiled.
5. Foiled on adhesive-backed batik.

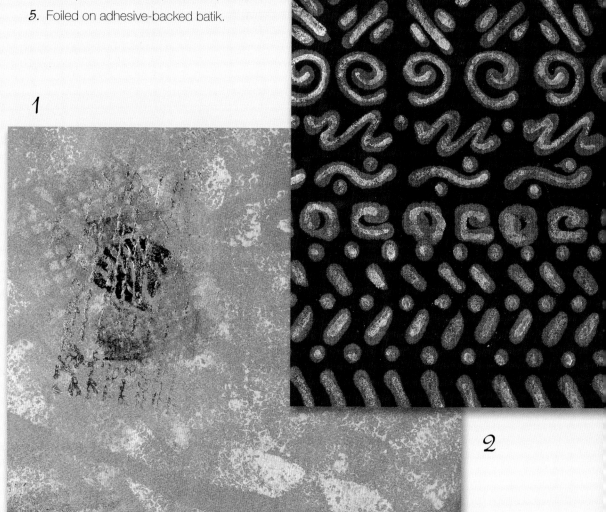

1

2

3

4

5

Note
It's a good idea to keep a notebook with sample swatches and list your steps if you wish to duplicate the fabric later. You can also scan your fabrics on the computer and print them out to keep a history of your creations.

N ow that you know all the different ways of embellishing the surface of fabrics, you're ready to turn them into delightful fabric beads. There are so many ways of making a fabric bead—and that's even before we start embellishing the finished beads!

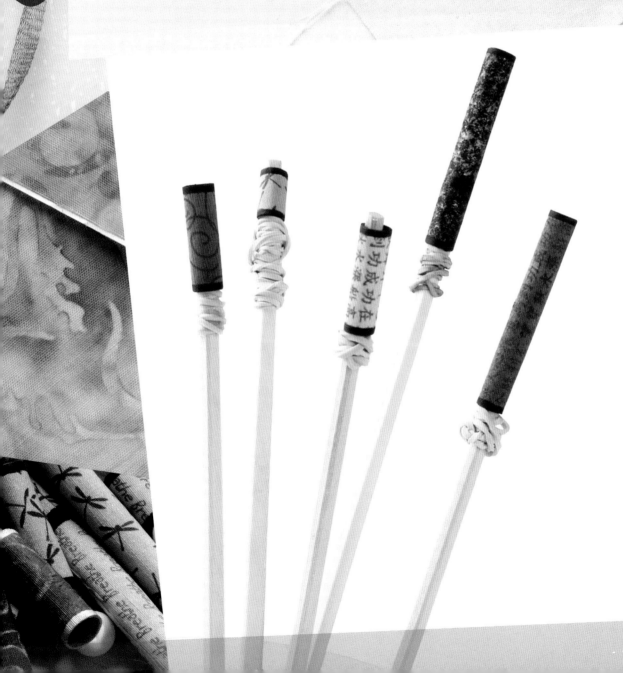

Cutting the Fabric

My favorite shapes of fabric beads are cylinders made from fabric cut in rectangles and thin ovals made from fabric cut in triangles. Use a rotary cutter, ruler, and mat for the speediest and most consistent fabric strips. Cut fabric strips with the grain going horizontally so that you cut with the grain, not against it. The longer the length of fabric, the more times it will wrap around a straw, making a stronger bead. I like my beads to be very sturdy and rigid, so I make the fabric lengths long (see chart below). Decide what straw size you want to use before cutting your fabric. Depending on the size of straw and stiffness of the fabric, you may need to cut longer or shorter pieces of certain fabrics.

The following are some common straw sizes and my recommendations for bead lengths. Feel free to venture out on your own and experiment!

+ Thin coffee stirrers: Cut fabric strips in 1½–2" (3.8–5 cm) lengths
+ Regular straws: Cut fabric strips in 3" (7.5 cm) lengths
+ Jumbo straws: Cut fabric strips in 5–6" (12.5–15 cm) lengths

Fabric rectangles

This shape bead has the strongest structure and is quite durable. Only the end of the fabric will show once you've rolled the bead into a cylinder. Depending on the diameter of the straw, you may only need to embellish 1" (2.5 cm) of the fabric. If you're foiling or stamping, you only need to cover the part that will show once the bead is rolled.

Supplies

× Fabric
× Cutting mat and rotary cutter
× Ruler

1. Cut one strip the width of the fabric along the grain to the desired length.

2. Cut this strip lengthwise to the desired widths. My favorites are ½" (1.3 cm), 1" (2.5 cm), 1½" (3.8 cm), and 2" (5 cm).

Triangles

This shape shows off a lot of edge, which can give your beads great visual texture.

Supplies

✘ Fabric
✘ Cutting mat and rotary cutter
✘ Ruler

Note
You can use the side pieces to make tiny matching beads.

1. Cut one strip the width of the fabric along the grain to the desired length.

2. Cut this strip lengthwise into the desired widths.

3. Leaving the edges straight for about ½" (1.3 cm), lay the ruler from the edge of the strip to the center of the opposite end and cut. Repeat for the opposite edge to form a centered point.

Drying Rack

A chopstick drying rack is very valuable to prevent smudging when embellishing or drying your beads. Knitting needles also work for this purpose.

Supplies

✘ Rubber bands
✘ Chopsticks
✘ Cup or other tall-sided container
✘ Dry beans or rice

1. Wrap a rubber band several times around a chopstick.

2. Slide bead over chopstick and be sure the rubber band fits snugly inside the bead.

3. Fill the small container with dry beans or uncooked rice. Place chopsticks in cup.

Rolling

Carefully rolling the fabric and lining up the edges is the key to a great finished bead. Remember, it's all about practice, practice, practice! In the beginning, you may want to practice on scrap fabric or paper. Over time, your beads will become consistent and look great. When rolling beads using light colors, use white paper or blank newsprint, not newspaper. Sometimes the ink rubs off on the bead.

Adhesive method

Think of this technique as making a big sticker, then cutting your fabric strips out of it. The straw stays inside the bead for stability. You will not be removing it later, so be sure the straw width is the same as your fabric strip width or the straw will show.

Supplies

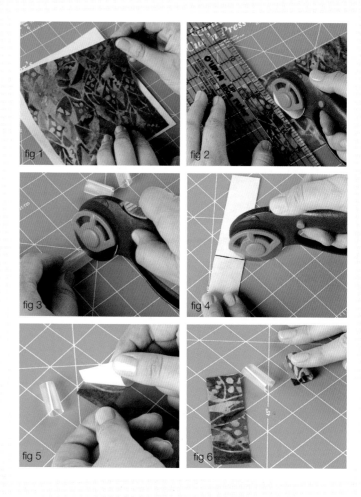

fig 1
fig 2
fig 3
fig 4
fig 5
fig 6

✕ Fabric
✕ Double Tack 2-sided mounting film (adhesive-backed paper)
✕ Cutting mat and rotary cutter
✕ Ruler

1. Cut a sheet of adhesive-backed paper slightly larger than your finished fabric.

2. Peel off one side of the paper and stick it to the back of your fabric (**Figure 1**), then trim edges.

3. Cut fabric to desired strips (**Figure 2**).

4. Cut straws to desired lengths (**Figure 3**).

5. Measure the length of fabric needed to cover one layer of the straw without overlapping the fabric. Mark length.

6. Cut the correct length of fabric (**Figure 4**).

7. Peel off the paper (**Figure 5**).

8. Roll fabric over a straw (**Figure 6**).

9. Dab edge of bead with glue to secure seam.

Gluing method

This is my favorite technique for most of my beads—it's quick and produces a strong stiff-sided bead. The straw is removed once the bead is dry, so you can cut the straw longer than the fabric width.

Supplies

- ✘ Fabric
- ✘ Straw
- ✘ Weldbond glue
- ✘ Spatula
- ✘ Newsprint or newspaper

1. Decide which size bead you want to make and cut your fabric accordingly. Place the fabric strip on top of newsprint right side down.

2. Fold end of fabric over straw to overlap rest of fabric and apply a line of glue to edge of fabric (**Figure 1**).

3. Use spatula to spread the glue evenly on the edge of the fabric strip (**Figure 2**).

4. Tuck glued edge under straw. Apply more glue to entire strip (**Figure 3**).

5. Spread glue evenly with spatula.

6. Carefully roll straw to the edge (**Figure 4**).

7. Roll the edge back and forth a few times to secure the seam (**Figure 5**).

   WALK AWAY FROM THE BEAD! While the bead is wet, resist the temptation to play with it. It can easily lose its shape or become lopsided if it's handled while wet. Just go make another one, or two, or three. . . .

8. Let dry.

9. Use the same process to make the triangle beads, spreading glue toward the point and rolling evenly (**Figures 6 and 7**).

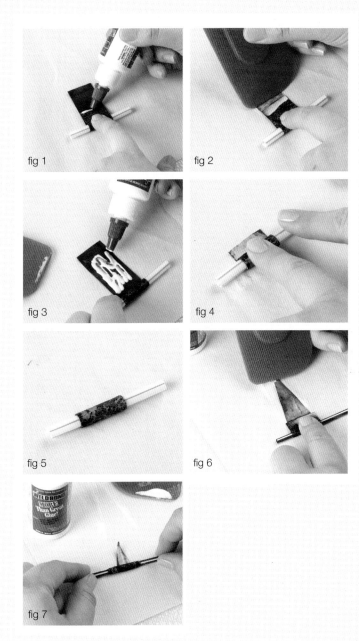

fig 1

fig 2

fig 3

fig 4

fig 5

fig 6

fig 7

Dipping

To dip or not to dip . . . that is the question! Dipping the ends of the bead in acrylic paint is an optional step. I think it gives the bead a more refined and finished appearance. By adding a layer of paint to the edges, it also increases the bead's strength. The paint color can dramatically change the look of your finished bead, so experiment with this technique. My favorite dipping colors are gold, silver, bronze, and copper. The keys to dipping are the consistency of the paint and how steady your hand is—so you may want to skip that extra cup of coffee before you dip!

Supplies

- ✘ Bead
- ✘ Acrylic paint
- ✘ Water
- ✘ Plastic bottle cap

1. Trim any stray fibers off the bead before dipping.

2. Fill the bottle cap halfway with the desired paint color.

3. Check the consistency of the paint; it should be like whole milk. If the paint is too thin, it will run; if it's too thick, it will be very difficult to get an even rim on the bead edge. If needed, add a drop or two of water to the cap and stir to mix evenly.

4. Holding the bead at one end, carefully dip the other end into the paint straight on, not at an angle (Figure 1).

5. Lift the bead straight up and allow to dry. Repeat for the other end.

Note

You may find using tweezers to hold the bead as you dip easier than holding the bead with your fingers, especially for short beads.

Stabilizing

Due to the large holes of these beads, they may need to be stabilized for stringing so they're not wobbly on your beading wire or head pin. Slide a 6–8mm plastic bead inside the fabric bead so that the holes run parallel to the fabric bead. When stringing, pass the beading wire or head pin through the plastic bead.

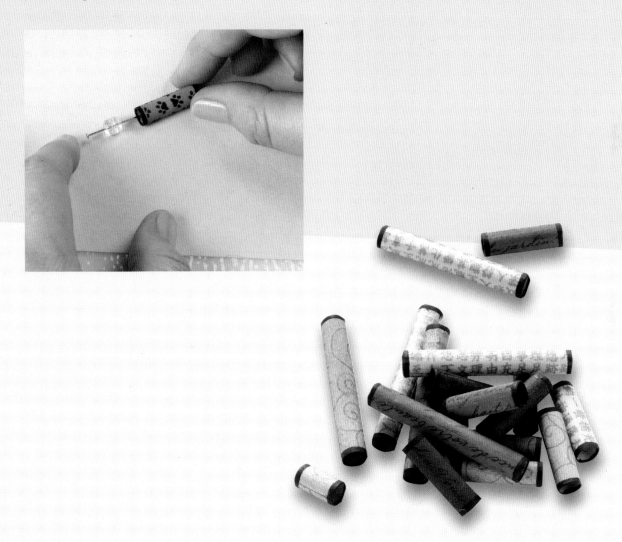

$\mathcal{V}$arious types of basic fabric beads have been around a long time, but I wanted to push the envelope and see how classy and sophisticated fabric beads could become. Once you start making these little beauties, your imagination will fly! You can make fabric beads as simple or as ornate as you desire. Many of these fabric "recipes" haven't been done before and may seem like a stretch, but I assure you that once you start creating, the fabric choices, textures, and surface treatments will keep you endlessly entertained!

IT'S ALL ABOUT THE FABRIC

Batik Beauties and Vintage Kimono

I love anything batik! Use adhesive-backed batiks or make your own (see page 13). Use vintage kimono panels or scraps to make one-of–a-kind vintage beads. Some vintage fabrics have stains or holes, which remind me of the rich life they led before ending up in my hands. Embellish or disguise any stains in your fabric by adding a splash of foil or Paintstiks.

Batik Bead Supplies

- ✕ Adhesive-backed batik fabric (commercial or prepared at home)
- ✕ Weldbond glue
- ✕ Straws
- ✕ Cutting mat and rotary cutter
- ✕ Ruler

Follow the instructions for making basic fabric beads using the adhesive method (see page 48).

Vintage Kimono Bead Supplies

- ✕ Vintage kimono fabric
- ✕ Cutting mat and rotary cutter
- ✕ Ruler
- ✕ Weldbond glue
- ✕ Straw
- ✕ Spatula

Follow the directions for gluing basic fabric beads (see page 49).
If the fabric is really thin, you may have to make your strips longer than usual.

Wedding and Name Beads

These beads make wonderful wedding jewelry—have a make-your-own-jewelry party for the bridal shower. I always use silk for wedding beads, as it has such an elegant sheen. Instead of a wedding, these beads can feature someone's name for a special event.

Supplies

- ✗ Fabric
- ✗ Paints
- ✗ Foam brush
- ✗ Freezer paper
- ✗ Computer and printer
- ✗ Weldbond glue
- ✗ Acrylic sealer
- ✗ Straws
- ✗ Cutting mat and rotary cutter
- ✗ Ruler
- ✗ Spatula

1. Follow directions on page 24 to paint the fabric. I like metallic taupe, champagne, and pearl white paint for these beads.

2. Create and format the words you want to print on your beads. Print them out on a sheet of paper and make a practice bead (Figure 1). Play with the spacing if necessary to make sure the words will appear as you intended.

3. When you are satisfied that the size and spacing are correct, follow the directions for computer printing (see page 41) to print on the silk fabric. Cut the fabric strips (Figure 2).

4. Roll the fabric over the straw and glue as described in the basic glued-bead method (see page 49).

5. Dip bead ends in a complementary color (see page 50). If desired, embellish with flatback crystals or tiny seed beads (see pages 74–75).

fig 1

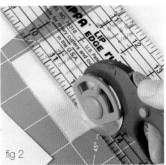

fig 2

Wooden Beads

Wooden beads come in a huge variety of shapes and sizes. Don't worry if you don't like the color—this collage technique covers the entire bead so the color won't show when you're done. This is a great project for your favorite fabric scraps.

Supplies

- ✖ Fabric
- ✖ Cutting mat and rotary cutter
- ✖ Small paintbrush
- ✖ Mod Podge
- ✖ Wooden beads
- ✖ Permanent metallic pen

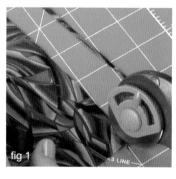
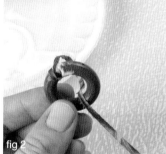

1. Cut thin strips of fabric (Figure 1).

2. Using a small paintbrush, coat a section of the bead with Mod Podge. Lay the fabric on the Mod Podge and wrap it in overlapping strips (Figure 2). Brush a layer of Mod Podge on top of the fabric. Repeat until bead is completely covered and let dry. (You may find it easier to manage if you slide your bead onto a chopstick or pencil.)

3. Cover entire bead with 2–4 layers of Mod Podge, allowing each layer to dry between coats.

4. Once the bead is completely dry, use a metallic pen to outline the rim of the bead.

Picture Resin Beads

Who can resist putting her pet's mug on a bead? Bow wow. . . . Works great for babies, too!
You can use this technique to decorate resin beads with other smooth, flat fabrics.

Supplies

- ✗ Solid light-colored fabric
- ✗ Computer and printer
- ✗ Acrylic sealant spray
- ✗ Scissors
- ✗ Small paintbrush
- ✗ Mod Podge
- ✗ Large flat-sided resin beads
- ✗ Metallic pen
- ✗ Flatback crystals and glue (optional)

fig 1

fig 2

fig 3

fig 4

1. Size an image on your computer to fit your bead. Follow the directions for computer printing (see page 41) to print out your picture and seal with acrylic spray. Cut out the image (Figure 1).

2. Using a small paintbrush, coat the top of the resin bead with Mod Podge (Figure 2).

3. Lay the image on top of the Mod Podge (Figure 3). Brush a layer of Mod Podge on top of the fabric and bead and let dry.

4. Add 2–4 layers of Mod Podge on top of the image, allowing the bead to dry between coats (Figure 4).

5. (Optional) Embellish by gluing crystal flatbacks onto bead front and sides (Figure 5).

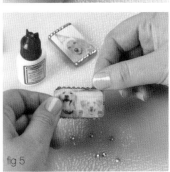
fig 5

MIXED MEDIA

Talisman Message Beads

This is my version of a message in a bottle! Have a fun time picking out sparkly fabrics with glitter or sequins in the fabric for a more dramatic effect.

Supplies

- ✗ Fabric
- ✗ Cutting mat and rotary cutter
- ✗ Clear plastic tubing
- ✗ Scissors
- ✗ 2 flat disc beads that will cover the tube ends securely
- ✗ 2-part epoxy (30-minute version)
- ✗ 1 head or eye pin
- ✗ 2 crystals
- ✗ Round-nose pliers
- ✗ Wire cutter
- ✗ Flat-nose pliers

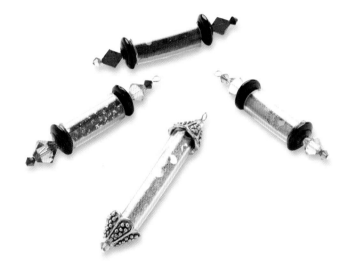

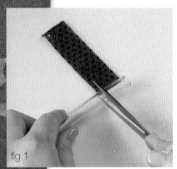

fig 1

fig 2

fig 3

fig 4

1. Use sharp scissors to cut tubing to desired length. Try to cut the edges as straight as possible (Figure 1).

2. Cut fabric to the width of the tube and 3" (7.5 cm) long (Figure 2).

3. Mix up the 2-part epoxy according to manufacturer's instructions.

4. Spread a little epoxy on one flat side of a bead and stick it to one end of the tube. Let dry (Figure 3).

5. Roll up fabric and slide inside tube.

6. On a head or eye pin, string 1 crystal, the glued tube with the epoxied side down, the remaining flat bead, and the remaining crystal (Figure 4). Finish head pin with a simple loop (see page 107).

Note

Write a special word, phrase, secret wish, or intention and slip it inside tube before you finish up. Shh— it's our little secret . . .

Princess Resin Beads

This is a quick and easy method of encasing fabric and flatback crystals in resin. You can drop almost any kind of three-dimensional items into the resin before it sets. The finished beads have a lovely shiny surface.

Supplies

- ✗ Fabric
- ✗ Blank picture pendant
- ✗ Scissors
- ✗ 2-part epoxy (resin)
- ✗ Paper plate
- ✗ Toothpick
- ✗ Permanent ink pad
- ✗ Crown stamp
- ✗ Weldbond glue
- ✗ Flatback crystals

fig 1

fig 2

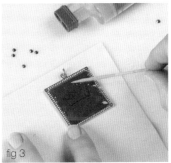
fig 3

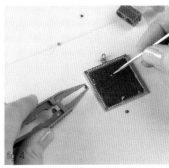
fig 4

1. Decorate fabric using techniques in Surface Design chapter. I used sponging for the background design and stamped a crown onto dried fabric.

2. Trace and cut out image to fit pendant (Figure 1).

3. Dab a tiny dot of glue onto the pendant surface and place the fabric on top of the glue. Smooth out with your finger if necessary.

4. On your paper plate, use the toothpick to mix up the 2-part epoxy according to manufacturer's instructions.

5. Use the toothpick to scoop up the epoxy and fill the pendant chamber with the epoxy (Figure 2).

6. Smooth the surface of the epoxy with the toothpick (Figure 3).

7. Using tweezers, carefully drop the flatback crystals as desired. Use a toothpick to poke out any air bubbles or reposition the crystals if needed (Figure 4).

8. Gently tap the pendant a couple of times on a flat surface, then let it set according to manufacturer's instructions.

Wire and Seed Bead Wrap

This is a great project to use up your orphan beads, crystals, and charms in an easy way to embellish fabric beads. I like to start with a jumbo fabric bead for this project.

Supplies

- ✖ Basic jumbo fabric bead
- ✖ Fabric trim
- ✖ Weldbond glue
- ✖ Craft wire
- ✖ Wire cutter
- ✖ Assorted seed beads, crystals, and charms

Note
You can use stretchy clear beading filament instead of craft wire to wrap the bead.

fig 1

fig 2

fig 3

fig 4

1. Glue trim around bead edges, trim, and let dry (Figure 1).

2. String craft wire with beads, crystals, and charms.

3. Wrap wire end around fabric bead and twist end onto itself like a twist tie (Figure 2).

4. Continue wrapping wire around bead and sliding beads where you like. It's interesting to leave spaces unbeaded so just the wire shows and the beads can slide around (Figure 3).

5. Finish end by twisting end onto itself and trim excess (Figure 4).

Crystal Edge Wrap

This is a little more complex than wrapping beads on the outside, but adding crystals to the edges of the fiber bead gives a polished look. The basic bead needs to be large enough for a hole punch to fit inside.

Supplies

- ✗ Basic jumbo fabric bead
- ✗ Small-hole punch
- ✗ Stretchy clear beading filament or wire
- ✗ Wire cutter or scissors
- ✗ Crystals or seed beads

fig 1

fig 2

fig 3

fig 4

1. Punch holes evenly around the edges of the fabric bead (Figure 1).

2. String beading filament or wire through a hole and tie a knot (Figure 2).

3. String 3–4 crystals or seed beads onto the filament or wire and slip the filament or wire through the next hole, passing from the inside to outside of the bead. Pull tight (Figure 3).

4. Repeat Step 3 until you have passed through all the holes on one end of the bead. Tie a knot in the filament or wire to secure and trim the end.

5. Repeat Steps 2–4 for the other end of the bead (Figure 4).

Hammered Copper Strips

The possibilities are endless with these copper strips.
Watch the edges—they can be pretty sharp.

Supplies

- ✗ Completed basic fabric bead
- ✗ Copper sheets
- ✗ Decorative scissors
- ✗ Embossing gun
- ✗ Permanent ink pad
- ✗ Rubber stamp
- ✗ Textured hammer
- ✗ Teflon sheet
- ✗ Mouse pad
- ✗ Weldbond glue
- ✗ Metal file

fig 1

fig 2

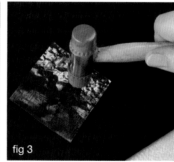
fig 3

fig 4

fig 5

1. Cut copper sheet long enough to wrap a strip around your bead. I like work with a 5–6" (12.5–15 cm) sheet to make a bunch of strips at the same time.

2. Stamp onto copper sheet using permanent ink and rubber stamp (Figure 1).

3. Heat copper sheet with an embossing gun (Figure 2). The color of the copper will change from bright copper to pink to lilac to silver; stop when you are happy with the color.

4. Place the copper on top of a mouse pad and hammer to add texture (Figure 3).

5. Using decorative scissors, cut thin strips of copper (Figure 4). File edges with a metal file if they're too sharp.

6. Glue copper strip onto fabric bead. Let dry (Figure 5).

Note

Make your own textured hammer by dropping globs of glue from a glue gun onto the head of a hammer.

Wire Lace Beads

Wire lace is really fun to work with. This ribbon is actually a tube of very fine knitted wire that you can stretch into waves, knot, and reshape. Experiment and design your own stunning creation!

Supplies

- ✘ Completed basic fabric bead
- ✘ Wire lace
- ✘ 2" (5 cm) length of beading wire, any size (to use for stringing)
- ✘ Crystals
- ✘ Super glue

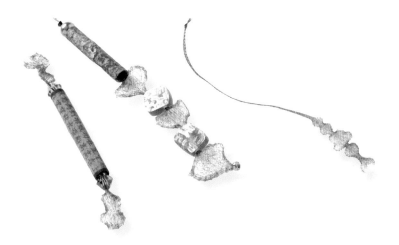

fig 1

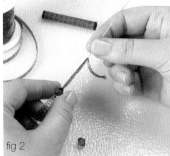
fig 2

fig 3

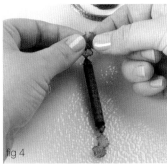
fig 4

1. Cut a piece of wire lace 4" (10 cm) longer than your finished bead (Figure 1).

2. To use the beading wire as a needle, fold the ends together with the wire lace inside the fold. String a crystal onto the wire lace (Figure 2).

3. String bead onto the wire lace (Figure 3).

4. String a crystal onto the wire lace.

5. Hold the sides of the wire lace and pull gently to create waves or flares (Figure 4).

6. Add a dab of glue where the wire lace meets each crystal to secure the lace.

Leather and Eyelet Beads

Visit your favorite scrapbooking or crafting store and pick up some eyelets for this project. They come in the sassiest colors and shapes! These beads will be glued and rolled, so you won't need to use straws—just roll the strips up like a jelly roll.

Supplies

- ✖ Leather
- ✖ Small-hole punch
- ✖ Eyelets
- ✖ Hammer
- ✖ Eyelet tool
- ✖ Weldbond glue
- ✖ Cutting mat and rotary cutter
- ✖ Ruler

fig 1

fig 2

fig 3

1. Cut strips of leather to the desired length and width.

2. Punch holes where you want to insert eyelets (Figure 1). Remember only the very end of the strip will show, so place eyelets at the end of the strip.

3. Place eyelet in hole, position eyelet tool properly into eyelet, and pound with a hammer (Figure 2).

4. Cover the back of the strip with glue and roll up (see page 49) (Figure 3). Let dry.

Embossed Leather Beads

Embossing on leather is the same as embossing on paper. The end result is a very rich effect. The bead edges of this project butt up against each other and only wrap once around the straw with no overlap.

Supplies

- ✕ Straw
- ✕ Leather strips
- ✕ Cutting mat and rotary cutter
- ✕ Rubber stamps
- ✕ Embossing powder
- ✕ Embossing ink pad
- ✕ Heat gun
- ✕ Weldbond glue
- ✕ Teflon sheet
- ✕ Ruler
- ✕ Small paint brush

fig 1

fig 2

fig 3

fig 4

1. Cut straw to desired length. Cut strip of leather the same width as the straw.

2. Stamp the leather using embossing ink (Figure 1).

3. Sprinkle embossing powder onto stamped image (Figure 2).

4. Tap off excess powder (Figure 3). Gently brush away any stray powder with a small paint brush.

5. Heat with embossing gun until powder has melted (Figure 4).

6. Wrap strip around straw once and cut at end so both edges of the leather butt up against each other when wrapped around the straw.

7. Lay leather strip right side down and spread glue all over the strip. Roll strip around straw (Figure 5).

8. Seal edges with a small line of glue and let dry.

fig 5

FIBER

Wild Fiber Beads

With all the wonderful fibers on the market, you can make beads to match everything in your wardrobe (and don't forget your friends')! This is a great way to use up any fabric beads you don't love, since they'll be completely covered in fiber.

Supplies

- ✗ Basic fabric bead
- ✗ Novelty yarn
- ✗ Scissors
- ✗ Weldbond glue
- ✗ Chopstick and rubber band

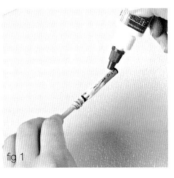
fig 1

fig 2

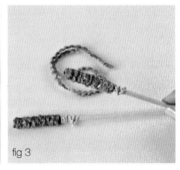
fig 3

1. Paint the basic bead to give the fabric a sturdier body. Dipping the bead ends is optional depending on the type of fiber you use—if you use fluffy fiber, the edges won't show, so don't bother dipping the bead ends.

2. Slip the bead onto a chopstick, securing the rubber band inside the bead so it won't slip.

3. Holding the chopstick, cover the entire bead with a thin layer of glue (Figure 1).

4. Beginning at one end, wrap the fiber strand around the bead in close coils so that none of the underlying bead shows through. Make sure the fiber is securely glued to the bead (Figure 2).

5. Trim end of fiber and push into the glue to secure. Let dry (Figure 3).

Angelina Fiber Beads

These beads are made from a beautifully iridescent thin fiber that can be made into a fabric.
The variations that are possible when you mix colors are really spectacular.

Supplies

- ✖ Angelina fibers
- ✖ Cutting mat and rotary cutter
- ✖ Ruler
- ✖ Iron
- ✖ Straw
- ✖ Teflon sheet or parchment paper
- ✖ Weldbond glue

Note

These are fun to
embellish with flatbacks
(see page 74).

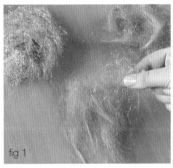

fig 1

fig 2

fig 3

fig 4

1. Lay out strands of Angelina on top of each other in several layers. I like to use 2–4 different-colored strands in the same piece (Figure 1).

2. Place Teflon sheet on top of fiber and iron according to Angelina manufacturer's instructions.

3. Cut strips out of the fiber sheet (see page 46) and follow the directions for rolling the basic glued-fabric bead (see page 48) (Figure 2).

4. Leave your bead on the straw to dry (Figure 3). When dry, slip bead off straw and trim edges (Figure 4). If the bead doesn't slip off the straw easily, slide small scissors along the inside of the bead and cut the straw out.

Fringed Beads

These beads make great pendants as well as curtain ties, lamp pulls, and other home décor projects.

Supplies

- ✘ Basic fabric bead
- ✘ Weldbond glue
- ✘ Paints
- ✘ Dangle trim or fringe
- ✘ Scissors
- ✘ Drying rack

1. Paint the basic bead to give the fabric a sturdier body. Dipping the bead ends is optional depending on the type of trim you use.

2. Slip the bead onto a chopstick, securing the rubber band inside the bead so it won't slip.

3. Cover the bead with a thick layer of glue (Figure 1). Wrap fringe around the bead, starting at one end of the bead and making sure the fringe is securely glued to the bead. Overlap about ¼" (6 mm) at the end of the bead (Figure 2). You may have to push and tug at the fringe to get it to lie properly; be sure to do this when the glue is still wet. Trim end of fiber and push into the glue to secure. Let dry.

fig 1

fig 2

variation

Some commercial trims have loops—customize them with your own dangles! Glue trim around both bead edges and let dry, then create dangles by stringing beads onto eye pins and attaching them onto the trim loops using your pliers. See page 107 for wireworking directions.

Ribbon Beads

The variety of ribbon colors and styles these days makes this project very versatile and exciting. Ribbon beads add great texture to any jewelry project.

Supplies

- ✘ Ribbons
- ✘ Straws
- ✘ Double Tack (2-sided mounting film)
- ✘ Scissors

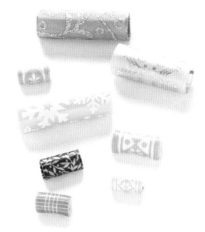

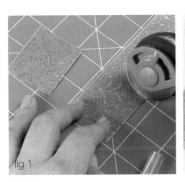

fig 1

fig 2

1. Cut ribbon to desired length; I use a 2" (5 cm) length for each bead (Figure 1).

2. Follow the directions for the basic adhesive fabric bead (see page 48) to adhere the mounting film to the back of the ribbon. Several widths of ribbon can be laid on the adhesive and cut later.

3. Remove paper backing and wrap strip around a straw (Figure 2).

4. Secure the seam with a dab of glue and let dry.

Note
You can also stamp designs on blank ribbons using permanent ink or paints.

STITCHED

Mini-quilt Beads

This is a great project to use up your quilt fabric scraps! Embellish them with more beads and crystals if you like.

Supplies

- ✗ Cutting mat and rotary cutter
- ✗ Ruler
- ✗ Fabric
- ✗ Batting
- ✗ Thread
- ✗ Sewing machine or handsewing needle
- ✗ Scissors
- ✗ Pins
- ✗ Weldbond glue
- ✗ Spatula

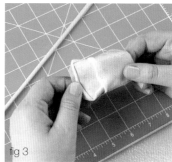

fig 1 fig 2 fig 3

1. Cut 2 pieces of fabric and 1 piece of batting to the same size; I cut them 4½" (11.5 cm) long by 2½" (6.5 cm) wide (Figure 1).

2. Place both pieces of fabric together with the right sides facing each other. Place the batting under the fabric pieces. Pin all three layers together.

3. Sew the pieces together on three sides, leaving one short end open. Clip the corners outside the seam, being careful not to cut the thread (Figure 2).

4. Turn inside out (Figure 3).

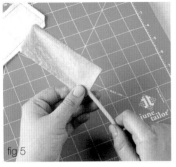
fig 5

fig 6

5. Use a chopstick to poke out the corners. (Figure 5)

6. Sew a decorative stitch (like the stipple stitch shown above).

7. Roll the fabric over the straw and glue following the basic glued-bead method (see page 49). (Figure 6)

Note
You can use a variety of stitches to create different effects.

Cross-stitched Beads

Here's an opportunity to use cross-stitch canvas in a whole new way.
Create an adorable fob for your favorite scissors.

Supplies

- ✗ Cross-stitch canvas
- ✗ Needle
- ✗ Cross-stitch thread
- ✗ Scissors
- ✗ Weldbond glue
- ✗ Spatula

1. Cut cross-stitch canvas in strips 2½" (6.5 cm) long and 1" (2.5 cm) wide.

2. Cross-stitch a simple design. (Figure 1).

3. Roll the fabric over the straw and glue following the basic glued-bead method (see page 49).

fig 1

Ribbon Muslin Bead

I love drooling over the fancy ribbon trims in the stores these days. I buy them all the time, but I had no idea what to do with them. It's wonderful to be able to wear them in an original creation!

Supplies

- ✕ Muslin
- ✕ Scissors
- ✕ Weldbond glue
- ✕ 2–4 colors of paint
- ✕ Sponge
- ✕ Coffee-stirrer-size straw
- ✕ Ribbon trim

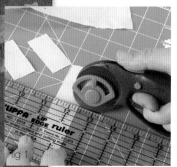

fig 1

fig 2

fig 3

fig 4

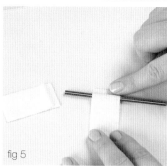

fig 5

1. Cut out 6 equal rectangles of muslin the same size as your desired finished bead (Figure 1). I cut them 1 x 2" (2.5 x 6.5 cm).

2. Brush a thin layer of glue on top of one muslin piece (Figure 2). Place a second piece of muslin on top of the glue (Figure 3). Repeat Step 2 two more times.

3. Place a small coffee stirrer on the top layer of muslin near one end and brush glue on the muslin layer, avoiding the straw. This creates a bail (Figure 4).

4. Place a piece of muslin on top of the glue and over the straw. Press down (Figure 5).

fig 6

fig 7

fig 8

fig 9

5. Repeat Step 2. Let dry.

6. Paint a solid base coat on the muslin bead. Let dry (Figure 6).

7. Use sponging technique (see page 26) to decorate the muslin (Figure 7). Let dry.

8. Paint the sides and back.

9. Cut a piece of ribbon trim the length of your bead (Figure 8).

10. Squeeze a stripe of glue the length of the muslin bead. Press the ribbon into the glue and let dry (Figure 9).

Square Muslin Bead

Use any kind of fabric you like for the top layer of this bead.
Then add some final touches of bling if you wish.

Supplies

- ✗ Muslin
- ✗ Scissors
- ✗ Weldbond glue
- ✗ Paints
- ✗ Sponge
- ✗ Coffee-stirrer-size straw
- ✗ Fabric
- ✗ Flatback crystals

1. Follow the directions for the Ribbon Muslin Bead, cutting 6 squares of muslin fabric. Place the straw across one corner diagonally so that the finished bead will hang in an even diamond shape.

2. Cut a colored print or custom-designed fabric for the top layer of fabric.

3. Paint the sides and back and embellish with crystals if desired.

FINISHING TOUCHES

Crystal Edges

These are great if you love bling! Here are three different methods to add sparkle to your beads.

Supplies

- ✖ Completed basic fabric bead
- ✖ Weldbond glue
- ✖ Flatback crystals
- ✖ Toothpick
- ✖ Tweezers

Note

You can also use a special hot-fix tool and hot-fix flatbacks instead of glue to attach flatback crystals to your bead.

fig 1   fig 2

1. Use a toothpick to dab a ring of glue around the end of the bead.

2. Holding flatbacks with tweezers, place them on top of the glue one by one (Figure 1). Use the tweezers to tap them in place (Figure 2).

3. Repeat with the other end of the bead.

variation

Why stop there? Dab glue and attach crystals in random designs on the bead or place the bead on a chopstick, dab glue all over it in rows, and cover the bead with wall-to-wall flatbacks!

Tiny Seed Bead Dipped Edges

What a fun easy embellishment! The smaller the beads, the better.

Supplies

✗ Completed basic fabric bead
✗ Weldbond glue
✗ Beadazzles (micro or mini-micro beads)

1. Squeeze line of glue around one edge of the bead (Figure 1).
2. Dip glued edge into container of beads (Figure 2). Tap off excess beads and let dry (Figure 3).
3. Repeat on the other side. Let dry.

fig 1

fig 2

fig 3

Paint-Dotted Beads

There are lots of fun fabric paint colors that come in bottles so you can easily control how much paint you squeeze out. This is a great way to jazz up a slightly boring bead.

Supplies

✗ Completed basic fabric bead
✗ Fabric paint

1. Dab dots of fabric paint all over the bead (Figure 1).
2. Let dry.

fig 1

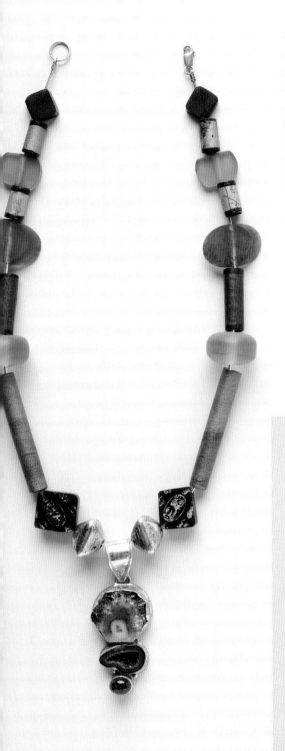

ow that you have piles and piles of fabric beads in every size, shape, and color, whatever will you do with them? Wear them, for starters! The following thirteen projects use fabric beads in a variety of different jewelry styles. The gallery that follows shows more jewelry ideas as well as other uses for your fabric bead treasures.

Mixed-Media Medley

I love these "mixed-media" earrings! The combination of metals, fiber, and silk beads make these a truly unique creation.

Supplies

- ✖ 2 lavender size 6° seed beads
- ✖ 6 silk ½" (1.3 cm) fabric beads, 2 each in teal, rust, and tan
- ✖ 4 peacock 4×10mm glass rondelles
- ✖ 2 silver 6mm coiled spacers
- ✖ 4 gold 2.5×10mm discs
- ✖ 2 silver 5×10mm tubes
- ✖ 2 silver 10mm spiral beads
- ✖ 2 silver 10mm metal bicones
- ✖ 2 copper 20×27mm flat diamond dangles
- ✖ 1 pair silver ear wires
- ✖ 6" (15 cm) of brown novelty yarn, cut in half
- ✖ 6" (15 cm) of green/blue novelty yarn, cut in half
- ✖ 6" (15 cm) of nylon ribbon yarn, cut in half
- ✖ Superglue
- ✖ Weldbond glue
- ✖ Scissors
- ✖ Chain-nose pliers

1. Use Weldbond to glue 1 rust silk bead to each metal dangle. Let dry for 24 hours.

2. Hold 1 strand of each fiber together and tie an overhand knot in the middle. Repeat with the remaining 3 strands.

3. Pass 1 group of knotted strands through 1 silk bead, centering the fiber to hide the knot inside the bead. Squeeze a dab of Weldbond glue inside the bead to secure the knot. Repeat with the remaining group of strands and silk bead. Let dry.

4. Use 1 end of one green/blue yarn to string 1 gold disc, 1 teal silk bead, and 1 gold disc. Tie an overhand knot. Use the other end of the yarn to string 1 spiral bead and tie an overhand knot. Repeat for the other earring so that it is a mirror image of the first.

5. Use the end of 1 brown yarn that is on the same side as the spiral bead to string 1 coiled spacer, 1 glass rondelle, 1 tan silk bead, 1 glass rondelle, and 1 silver tube. Tie an overhand knot. Use the other end of the yarn to string 1 silver bicone and tie an overhand knot. Repeat for the other earring so that it is a mirror image of the first.

6. Place a drop of superglue on the knots and let dry.

7. Use chain-nose pliers to open 1 ear-wire loop. String 1 seed bead and 1 dangle and close ear-wire loop. Repeat for the other earring.

Silver and Silk Trio

Classic sterling silver, silk, and complementary crystals—what could be better? It's like adding swinging fringe to your ears!

Supplies

- ✖ 4 teal/black ½" (1.3 cm) silk triangle beads
- ✖ 2 teal/black ¾" (2 cm) silk triangle beads
- ✖ 2 silver 25×22mm diamond chandelier findings
- ✖ 12 crystal 3mm crystal bicones
- ✖ 12 blue zircon 4mm crystal bicones
- ✖ 2 blue zircon chaton crystal round stones (size 1100 SS19)
- ✖ 4 silver 6mm jump rings
- ✖ 6 silver 1½" (3.8 cm) head pins
- ✖ 2 silver ear-post cups with backs
- ✖ 3" (7.6 cm) of silver 2mm chain
- ✖ 2-part epoxy
- ✖ Wire cutter
- ✖ Round-nose pliers
- ✖ Chain-nose pliers

1. Mix the 2-part epoxy according to manufacturer's instructions. Glue 1 chaton crystal into each ear-post cup. Let cure for 24 hours.

2. Use 1 head pin to string 1 crystal bicone, 1 blue zircon bicone, one ½" (1.3 cm) fabric bead, 1 blue zircon bicone, and 1 crystal bicone. Form a simple loop that attaches to 1 side loop of 1 chandelier finding. Repeat entire step three more times, attaching each head pin to 1 side loop of the chandelier findings.

3. Use 1 head pin to string 1 crystal bicone, 1 blue zircon bicone, one ¾" (2 cm) fabric bead, 1 blue zircon bicone, and 1 crystal bicone. Form a simple loop that attaches to the bottom loop of 1 chandelier finding. Repeat entire step for the other chandelier finding.

4. Use 1 jump ring to attach 1½" (3.8 cm) of chain to the top loop of 1 chandelier finding. Use 1 jump ring to attach the previous jump ring to 1 ear-post cup. Repeat entire step for the other earring.

Asian Posts

Create these elegant lightweight beauties in every color of the rainbow. Customize the matching crystal post to set off the foiled silk beautifully.

Supplies

- ✖ 2 black/red/gold 2" (5 cm) fabric triangle beads
- ✖ 4 light Colorado topaz 3mm crystal bicones
- ✖ 4 jet 4×6mm crystal bicone spacers
- ✖ 2 garnet chaton crystal round stones (size 1100 SS19)
- ✖ 2 gold ear-post cups with backs
- ✖ 2 gold 3" (7.5 cm) head pins
- ✖ 2-part epoxy
- ✖ Wire cutters
- ✖ Round-nose pliers
- ✖ Chain-nose pliers

1. Mix the 2-part epoxy according to manufacturer's instructions. Glue 1 chaton crystal into each ear-post cup. Let cure for 24 hours.

2. Use 1 head pin to string 1 crystal bicone, 1 crystal rondelle, 1 silk bead, 1 crystal rondelle, and 1 crystal bicone. Form a simple loop that attaches to 1 ear-post cup.

3. Repeat Step 2 for the second earring.

Wire Whimsy

It's fun to experiment with a variety of shapes when making these wire links. Each bracelet you create is one of a kind.

Supplies

- ✗ 6 gold matte size 8° seed beads
- ✗ 4 olive matte size 8° seed beads
- ✗ 5 batik 1" (2.5 cm) fabric triangle beads
- ✗ 10 crystal copper 2mm crystal bicones
- ✗ 10 jet 3mm crystal bicones
- ✗ 10 smoky topaz 4mm bicone crystals
- ✗ 5 jet 4×6mm crystal bicone spacers
- ✗ 5 natural brass 6mm flower spacers
- ✗ 8 natural brass 10mm twisted jump rings
- ✗ 15 gold 2" (5 cm) head pins
- ✗ 18" (45.5 cm) of gunmetal 18-gauge wire
- ✗ Hammer
- ✗ Steel block
- ✗ Wire cutter
- ✗ Round-nose pliers
- ✗ Chain-nose pliers

1. Cut wire into six 3" (7.5 cm) pieces. Use round-nose and chain-nose pliers to form each 3" (7.5 cm) piece of wire into a geometric link about ½–¾" (1.3–2 cm) wide by 1–1½" (2.5–3.8 cm) long. Repeat entire step, to form a total of 5 different links.

2. Use the fattest point of the round-nose pliers to grip 3" (7.5 cm) of wire 1½" (3.8 cm) from one end. Fold the wire 180° around the pliers. Repeat, using the midpoint of the pliers and gripping 1" (2.5 cm) from the other end of the wire. Form about half of a simple loop using the last ¼" (6 mm) of each end of wire to make an S-hook clasp.

3. Use the hammer and steel block to flatten the links formed in Step 1 and the hook formed in Step 2. Set aside.

4. Use 1 head pin to string 1 gold matte seed bead, 1 jet bicone, 1 flower spacer, 1 jet bicone, and 1 gold matte seed bead; form a simple loop. Repeat entire step twice more using gold matte seed beads and twice more using olive matte seed beads. Set aside.

5. Use 1 head pin to string 1 smoky topaz bicone, 1 silk bead, and 1 smoky topaz bicone; form a simple loop. Repeat entire step four times. Set aside.

6. Use 1 head pin to string 1 crystal copper bicone, 1 jet rondelle, and 1 crystal copper bicone; form a simple loop. Repeat entire step four times.

7. Use 1 jump ring to string 1 dangle each from Steps 4 through 6 and connect the hook to 1 link. Repeat four times, using 1 jump ring to string dangles and connect 1 link to the previous link.

8. Form a chain with the remaining 3 jump rings and attach 1 end of the chain to the final link.

Color Palettes

I like to take a simple color palette, add some varying shades of the same color, and throw in a surprising touch of another color to give it pizzazz. Layering color creates spectacular depths of hue and texture.

You can use these palettes to select supplies. Study the palette images you enjoy in this book and use it to shop for your projects by selecting components that match the colors in the palette picture. Notice how many different shades and colors are in the picture; feel free to add or subtract colors from the palette. I often use eight or nine different shades of a particular color in one project to give it a richer depth of color.

I like to include a bit of brass, gold, and silver in almost every jewelry design or palette. You don't have to worry about matching metals, especially in jewelry.

Blue

Blues make me think of the sky, ocean, sleep, and twilight. The ancient Egyptians used lapis lazuli to represent heaven. A pure blue is the color of inspiration, sincerity, and spirituality. I must admit blue is my favorite color palette. For a touch of variety, I added bronze, brass, and silver to this palette.

Note
You can wear this bracelet as is or twist it for a more textured look.

Delicado Bracelet

This delicate beauty weighs next to nothing and is quite easy to make. Use small scraps to make tiny fabric beads for this project.

Supplies

- ✗ 14 bronze assorted ¼–¾" (6–20mm) silk triangle beads
- ✗ 14 teal assorted ¼–¾" (6–20mm) silk triangle beads
- ✗ 14 purple assorted ¼–¾" (6–20mm) silk triangle beads
- ✗ 18 crystal copper 4mm crystal bicones
- ✗ 17 Capri blue 4mm crystal bicones
- ✗ 17 Montana 2XAB 4mm crystal bicones

- ✗ 4 crystal copper 4mm (size SS9) flatback crystals
- ✗ 1 silver 25mm 3-strand toggle clasp
- ✗ 6 silver 2mm crimp tubes
- ✗ 30" (76 cm) of .014 beading wire
- ✗ Crimping pliers
- ✗ Wire cutter
- ✗ Round-nose pliers
- ✗ Chain-nose pliers
- ✗ 2-part epoxy

1. Use 10" (25.5 cm) of beading wire to string 1 crimp tube and an outside loop of the ring half of the clasp. Pass back through the tube and crimp.

2. String 1 crystal copper bicone and 1 bronze silk bead fourteen times. String 4 crystal copper bicones, 1 crimp tube, and the outside loop of the bar half of the clasp. Pass back through the tube and crimp.

3. Use 10" (25.5 cm) of beading wire to string 1 crimp tube and the middle loop of the ring half of the clasp. Pass back through the tube and crimp. Repeat Step 2, using Capri blue bicones, teal silk beads, and the middle loop of the bar half of the clasp, making sure that the beaded strands do not twist.

4. Repeat Step 1 with the other outer loop of the toggle. Repeat Step 2, using Montana 2×AB bicones and purple silk beads.

5. Mix the 2-part epoxy according to manufacturer's instructions and glue crystal copper flatbacks to the ring half of the clasp. Let cure for 24 hours.

Color Palette

Purple

Purple and lavender are a favorite palette to play with. Purple encourages creativity and connection with your spiritual higher self as well as increased imagination and inspiration. I have added some indigo, pink, silver, and bronze to the mix along with a tad of fiber for a deeper, more complex color palette.

Mermaid Necklace

Take a unique trip to the seashore with this necklace! Mix seashells, pearls, and nuggets that evoke sea glass, then add an unexpected touch: a seafaring kitty focal bead.

Supplies

- ✕ 12 blue matte size 8° seed beads
- ✕ 16 blue matte size 6° seed beads
- ✕ 13 sea foam size 6° seed beads
- ✕ 2 teal ½" (1.3 cm) silk beads
- ✕ 6 teal 1" (2.5 cm) silk beads
- ✕ 12 crystal 4x6mm crystal bicone spacers
- ✕ 4 aquamarine 6mm crystal bicones
- ✕ 12 indicolite 8mm crystal bicones
- ✕ 10 Pacific opal 8mm crystal cubes
- ✕ 16 light gray 8mm crystal pearls
- ✕ 9 mottled turquoise 12mm Czech pressed-glass flat squares
- ✕ 10 shell 6x10mm beads
- ✕ 1 ceramic 14x45mm mermaid kitty bead
- ✕ 6 aqua 20–25mm resin nuggets
- ✕ 2 silver fold-over crimp ends
- ✕ 4 silver 2mm crimp tubes
- ✕ 22" (56 cm) of teal ⅝" (1.5cm) organza ribbon
- ✕ 40" (101.5 cm) of silver .019 beading wire
- ✕ Scissors
- ✕ Wire cutters
- ✕ Crimping pliers
- ✕ Flat-nose pliers

1. Use scissors to cut the ribbon in half. Use flat-nose pliers to attach 1 fold-over crimp end to one end of one ribbon. Repeat with the second crimp end and other ribbon.

2. Attach 19" (48.5 cm) of beading wire to the loop of one fold-over crimp end using a crimp tube. String 1 sea foam size 6° seed bead, 1 aquamarine 6mm bicone, 1 indicolite 8mm bicone, 1 size 8° seed bead, 1 aquamarine 6mm bicone, 1 sea foam size 6° seed bead, 1 shell bead, and 1 size 8° seed bead. String (1 Pacific opal cube, 1 sea foam size 6° seed bead, 1 indicolite 8mm bicone, 1 mottled turquoise flat square, 1 shell bead, and 1 size 8° seed bead) nine times. String 1 Pacific opal cube, 1 sea foam size 6°, 1 aquamarine 6mm bicone, 1 size 8° seed bead, 1 indicolite 8mm bicone, 1 aqua-marine 6mm bicone, 1 sea foam size 6°, 1 crimp tube, and the loop of the other fold-over crimp end. Pass back through the tube and crimp.

3. Attach 21" (53.5 cm) of beading wire to the loop of one fold-over crimp end using a crimp tube. String 1 blue matte size 6° seed bead, 1 light gray pearl, one ½" (1.3 cm) silk bead, 1 light gray earl, and 1 blue matte size 6° seed bead. String (1 crystal bicone spacer, 1 resin nugget, 1 crystal bicone spacer, 1 blue matte size 6° seed bead, 1 light gray pearl, one 1" (2.5 cm) silk bead, 1 light gray pearl, and 1 blue matte size 6° seed bead) three times.

4. String the mermaid kitty pendant. Repeat Step 3, reversing the stringing sequence and attaching the wire to the other fold-over crimp end.

5. Tie organza ribbon into a bow.

Color Palette

Aqua

Aqua is the color of high ideals. The combination of blue and green creates a very tranquil feeling. I threw in a hint of lavender and silver for a richer, more varied palette.

Dream Catcher

My mini version of a dream catcher, this necklace is guaranteed to keep nightmares away and peaceful thoughts flowing in!

Supplies

- ✗ 2 olivine size 6° seed beads
- ✗ 1 copper size 6° seed bead
- ✗ 7 bronze assorted ¼–⅔" (6–17 mm) silk triangle beads
- ✗ 6 light green 3mm crystal pearl rounds
- ✗ 4 light green 5mm crystal pearl rounds
- ✗ 2 bronze 4mm crystal pearl rounds
- ✗ 1×7 crystal copper 3mm crystal bicones
- ✗ 17 olivine 4mm crystal bicones
- ✗ 1 crystal copper 6mm crystal bicone
- ✗ 2 crystal copper 6mm crystal rounds
- ✗ 4 crystal copper 8mm crystal rounds
- ✗ 1 natural brass 18mm butterfly charm
- ✗ 1 copper 25mm hammered ring

- ✗ 1 natural brass 28×34mm delicate crest filigree
- ✗ 1 copper 7mm hammered ring
- ✗ 1 copper 25mm square toggle clasp
- ✗ 2 copper 2mm crimp beads
- ✗ 2 copper 4×6mm oval jump rings
- ✗ 2 copper 6mm jump rings
- ✗ 2 natural brass 6mm jump rings
- ✗ 1 natural brass 10mm twisted jump rings
- ✗ 9 natural brass 2" (5 cm) head pins
- ✗ 1 natural brass 1½" (3.8 cm) eye pin
- ✗ 18" (45.75 cm) of copper chain with 10mm round links
- ✗ 5" (13 cm) of copper .014 beading wire
- ✗ Wire cutter
- ✗ Chain-nose pliers
- ✗ Round-nose pliers

1. Use 1 head pin to string 1 crystal copper 3mm bicone, 1 olivine 4mm bicone, the largest silk bead, 1 olivine 4mm bicone, and 1 crystal copper 3mm bicone. Form a simple loop that attaches to the bottom hole of the delicate crest filigree. Repeat entire step six times, attaching each dangle to the delicate crest filigree and placing the silk beads from largest to smallest.

2. Use 1 head pin to string 1 olivine 4mm bicone, the copper seed bead, and 1 olivine 4mm bicone. Form a simple loop. Use 1 head pin to string 1 crystal copper 3mm bicone, 1 olivine seed bead, the 6mm crystal copper bicone, and 1 olivine 4mm bicone. Form a simple loop. Attach the eye pin to the butterfly charm. Use the eye pin to string 1 crystal copper 3mm bicone, 1 bronze crystal pearl, 1 olivine seed bead, 1 bronze crystal pearl, and 1 crystal copper 3mm bicone. Form a simple loop.

3. Use the twisted jump ring to string the 3 dangles formed in Step 2 (from shortest to longest), the copper 25mm hammered ring, and the top of the delicate crest filigree. Close the jump ring.

4. Cut the chain into one 8¼" (21 cm) piece (12 links) and one 9" (23 cm) piece (13 links). Attach 1 natural brass 6mm jump ring to one end of each chain.

5. Use the beading wire to string 1 crimp tube and the natural brass 6mm jump ring attached to the 8¼" (21 cm) chain. Pass back through the tube and crimp. String 1 light green 3mm crystal pearl, 1 crystal copper 6mm round, 1 light green 3mm crystal pearl, 1 crystal copper 8mm round, 1 light green 5mm crystal pearl, 1 crystal copper 8mm round, 1 light green 3mm crystal pearl, and 1 light green 5mm crystal pearl.

6. String the twisted jump ring used in Step 3. Repeat Step 5, reversing the stringing sequence and attaching the wire to the natural brass 6mm jump ring attached to the 9" (23 cm) chain.

7. Use 1 copper 6mm jump ring to attach the ring half of the toggle to the other end of the 9" chain. Use 1 copper 6mm jump ring to attach the hammered copper ring to the other end of the 8¼" (21 cm) chain. Attach 1 copper 4×6mm oval jump ring to the hammered copper ring. Use the remaining copper 4×6mm oval jump ring to connect the first oval jump ring to the bar half of the clasp.

Color Palette

Red

Red is associated with fiery heat and warmth. Reds represent life and vitality. I muted this palette a bit with pink, brass, gold, and black. Some red coral and a variety of pearls add a soft edge to the brilliance of the reds.

Floralessence

I love how the dangling dragonfly charm adds a third dimension to the shell pendant. The embellished resin slices create dramatic texture.

Supplies

- ✕ 5 matte olive size 8° seed beads
- ✕ 6 chartreuse ½" (1.3 cm) silk beads
- ✕ 3 light Colorado topaz 3mm crystal bicones
- ✕ 16 jet 3mm crystal bicones
- ✕ 3 olivine 4mm crystal bicones
- ✕ 2 smoky topaz 4mm bicone crystals
- ✕ 16 powder almond 4mm crystal pearls
- ✕ 12 dark gray 8mm crystal pearls
- ✕ 6 lime 15mm resin flat diamonds
- ✕ 1 pale green 30×40mm etched shell pendant
- ✕ 1 natural brass 4mm flower spacer
- ✕ 1 natural brass 18mm dragonfly charm
- ✕ 3 natural brass 1" (2.5 cm) head pins
- ✕ 1 natural brass 25mm water lily toggle ring
- ✕ 1 natural brass 6x30mm etched toggle bar
- ✕ 1 natural brass 4mm jump ring
- ✕ 1 natural brass 10mm twisted jump ring
- ✕ 2 gold-filled 2×3mm twisted crimp tubes
- ✕ 6" (15.5 cm) of natural brass 10mm round chain (20 links)
- ✕ 19" (48.5 cm) of brass .014 beading wire
- ✕ Small sponge
- ✕ Gold acrylic paint
- ✕ Silver acrylic paint
- ✕ Acrylic spray sealer
- ✕ Round-nose pliers
- ✕ Chain-nose pliers
- ✕ Wire cutters

1. Use the sponge and silver acrylic paint to lightly sponge both sides of the resin pieces. Let dry.

2. Repeat Step 1, using gold acrylic paint.

3. Spray the resin pieces with acrylic sealer.

4. Use 1 head pin to string 1 smoky topaz 4mm bicone, 1 seed bead, 1 light Colorado topaz 3mm bicone, the natural brass flower spacer, and 1 light Colorado topaz 3mm bicone. Form a simple loop that attaches to the bottom loop of the dragonfly pendant. Use 1 head pin to string 1 seed bead, 1 light Colorado topaz 3mm bicone, and 1 seed bead; form a simple loop. Use the 4mm jump ring to attach the simple loop to the top loop of the dragonfly link. Use the 10mm twisted jump ring to connect the 4mm jump ring to the shell pendant.

5. Use chain-nose pliers to separate the chain into two 3" (7.5 cm) pieces. Attach the last link of 1 chain to the toggle ring. Use 1 head pin to string the toggle ring and form a wrapped loop that attaches to the last link of the second chain.

6. Attach the beading wire to the other end of 1 chain using a crimp tube. String 1 seed bead, 1 olivine 4mm bicone, 1 jet 3mm bicone, and 1 powder almond pearl. String (1 jet bicone, 1 resin diamond, 1 jet bicone, 1 powder almond pearl, 1 dark gray pearl, 1 silk bead, 1 dark gray pearl, and 1 powder almond pearl) three times. String 1 jet bicone, 1 powder almond pearl, and 1 smoky topaz 4mm bicone.

7. String the twisted jump ring. Repeat Step 6, reversing the stringing sequence and attaching the wire to the other end of the second chain.

Color Palette

Brown

Browns are so earthy, symbolizing wholesomeness, nature, and dependability. I like to stretch my brown palette to include bronzes, golds, terracottas, coppers, silvers, and smoky blacks. The textures include laminated woods, amber crystals, and patinaed brass.

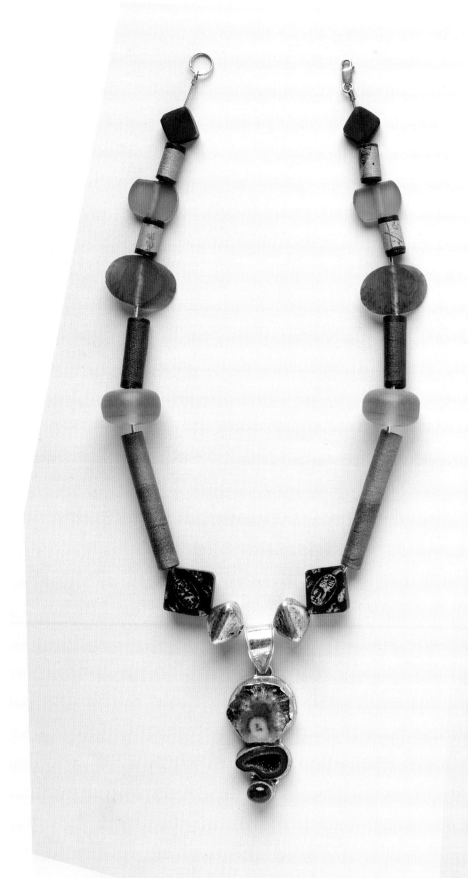

Amethyst Magic

Throwing in a splash of lime with the amethyst makes a bold vibrant statement. This necklace is not for the meek!

Supplies

- ✕ 2 purple ½" (1.3 cm) silk beads
- ✕ 2 lime ½" (1.3 cm) silk beads
- ✕ 2 purple 1" (2.5 cm) silk beads
- ✕ 2 purple 2" (5 cm) silk beads
- ✕ 2 purple 14mm resin diamonds
- ✕ 2 lime 14×18mm resin slices
- ✕ 2 purple 18×25mm resin ovals
- ✕ 2 lime 12×20mm resin rondelles
- ✕ 2 purple 22mm resin diamonds
- ✕ 2 silver 14mm square bicones
- ✕ 1 silver with amethyst inlay 25×70mm pendant with bail
- ✕ 1 silver 8mm split ring
- ✕ 1 sterling silver 18" (45.5 cm) omega chain with attached lobster clasp
- ✕ Silver acrylic paint
- ✕ Black StazOn ink pad (permanent) and cleaner
- ✕ Rubber stamps
- ✕ 1" (2.5 cm) foam brush
- ✕ Clear acrylic spray sealer
- ✕ Split ring tool

1. Use the foam brush to spread a thin layer of silver paint on a rubber stamp and stamp on the purple 22mm resin diamonds. Let dry. Repeat for back side.

2. Using StazOn ink pad, stamp on the purple resin ovals. Let dry. Repeat for back side.

3. Spray resin pieces with acrylic sealer.

4. Use the non-clasp end of the neck wire to string one 14mm resin diamond, 1 purple ½" (1.3 cm) silk tube, 1 resin slice, 1 lime ½" (1.3 cm) silk bead, 1 resin oval, 1 purple 1" (2.5 cm) silk bead, 1 resin rondelle, 1 purple 2" (5 cm) silk bead, one 22mm resin diamond, and 1 silver square bicone.

5. String the pendant. Repeat Step 4, reversing the stringing sequence.

6. Use the split ring tool to attach the split ring to the non-clasp end of the neck wire.

Green

Green signifies the powerful energies of nature and growth. Change and transformation are necessary for growth; this color can aid in these areas of life. This palette is based on an olive green with copper, silver, gold, yellow green, wood, and fiber in the mix.

Shimmering Silvers

Such a classy look with silver and crystal! This necklace offers an entirely different way to wear your fabric beads: vertically instead of horizontally.

Supplies

- ✖ 4 silver ½" (1.3 cm) silk beads
- ✖ 4 silver 1" (2.5 cm) silk beads
- ✖ 1 silver 2" (5 cm) silk bead
- ✖ 2 crystal AB 8mm crystal bicones
- ✖ 2 crystal 12×18 mm crystal rondelles
- ✖ 4 light gray 8mm crystal pearls
- ✖ 22 silver 5mm coiled spacers
- ✖ 2 silver 18×6mm double spiral beads
- ✖ 12 silver 2×15mm cornflake spacers
- ✖ 1 sterling silver 16" neck wire
- ✖ Fabric marker
- ✖ Ruler
- ✖ Dremmel tool

1. Measure and mark ½" (1.3 cm) from one end of each silk bead. Use the Dremmel tool to drill a small hole through each bead at its mark. (Be sure to use the drilled holes when stringing the silk beads.)

2. Use the neck wire to string 1 pearl, 1 coiled spacer, one ½" (1.3 cm) silk bead, 1 coiled spacer, 1 crystal AB bicone, 1 coiled spacer, one 1" (2.5 cm) silk bead, 1 coiled spacer, 1 pearl, 1 coiled spacer, one ½" (1.3 cm) silk bead, 1 coiled spacer, 1 double spiral bead, 1 coiled spacer, one 1" (2.5 cm) silk bead, 1 coiled spacer, 3 cornflake spacers, 1 coiled spacer, 1 crystal rondelle, 1 coiled spacer, 3 cornflake spacers, and 1 coiled spacer.

3. String the 2" (5 cm) silk bead. Repeat Step 2, reversing the stringing sequence.

Color Palette

Silver, White, and Gray

I love the cool combination of icy silvers, whites, and grays. A splash of crystals with the AB (aurora borealis) coating adds a lovely shimmer. This is a great palette for elegant wedding or holiday jewelry.

Ribbon Bead Necklace & Earrings

This is a simply elegant design. Classic yet contemporary—who would ever think these beads were made out of ribbon?

Necklace Supplies

- ✖ 99 crystal 3mm crystal bicones
- ✖ 50 smoky quartz 4mm crystal bicones
- ✖ 34 crystal AB 4mm crystal bicones
- ✖ 28 white alabaster 4mm crystal rounds
- ✖ 15 crystal copper 6mm crystal rounds
- ✖ 98 bronze 4mm round crystal pearls
- ✖ 28 light gray 8mm round crystal pearls
- ✖ 49 bronze 8×9mm twisted crystal pearls
- ✖ 14 cream ½" ribbon beads (see page 69)
- ✖ 1 sterling silver 16mm toggle clasp
- ✖ 2 sterling silver 6mm jump rings
- ✖ 6 sterling silver 2mm twisted crimp tubes
- ✖ 90" of .014 beading wire
- ✖ Wire cutters
- ✖ Crimping pliers
- ✖ Chain-nose pliers

Note

You can wear the necklace as is or twist the strands.

Earrings Supplies

- ✖ 4 crystal 3mm crystal bicones
- ✖ 4 light Colorado topaz 4mm crystal bicones
- ✖ 4 light gray 8mm crystal pearls
- ✖ 2 cream ribbon beads
- ✖ 2 silver ear wires
- ✖ 2 silver 2" head pins
- ✖ Wire cutters
- ✖ Round-nose pliers
- ✖ Chain-nose pliers

1. Use chain-nose pliers to attach 1 jump ring to each half of the clasp.

2. Use 30" (76 cm) of wire to string 1 crimp tube and 1 jump ring. Pass back through the tube and crimp using crimping pliers. Trim excess wire.

3. String one 3mm crystal bicone and one 4mm bronze round crystal pearl ninety-eight times. String one 3mm crystal bicone, 1 crimp tube, and the other jump ring. Pass back through the tube and crimp.

4. Repeat Step 2 using a second 30" (76 cm) wire.

5. String one 4mm smoky quartz bicone and 1 bronze twisted pearl forty-nine times. String one 4mm smoky quartz bicone, 1 crimp tube, and the other jump ring. Pass back through the tube and crimp.

6. Repeat Step 2 using the remaining 30" (76 cm) of wire.

7. String three 4mm crystal AB bicones. String 1 crystal copper round, one 4mm crystal AB bicone, 1 white alabaster round, 1 light gray crystal pearl, 1 ribbon bead, 1 light gray crystal pearl, 1 white alabaster round, and one 4mm crystal AB bicone fourteen times. String 1 crystal copper round, three 4mm crystal AB bicones, 1 crimp tube, and the other jump ring. Pass back through the tube and crimp.

8. Connect one end of each strand to the jump ring. Repeat for other side.

1. Use 1 head pin to string one 3mm crystal bicone, one 4mm light Colorado topaz crystal bicone, 1 light gray crystal pearl, 1 ribbon bead, 1 light gray crystal pearl, one 4mm light Colorado topaz bicone, and one 3mm crystal bicone.

2. Form a simple loop that attaches to 1 ear wire.

3. Repeat Steps 1 and 2 to make a second earring.

Color Palette

Pink

Pink is the color of universal love and can promote self-worth and beauty. This palette is full of a wide variety of shades of pink as well as silver, black, and a spot of coral.

Batik Beauty

Capture any piece of fabulous fabric inside these glass frames for a uniquely customized design and don't forget the matching fabric beads.

Supplies

- ✕ 9 copper size 6° seed beads
- ✕ 6 orange batik foiled 1" (2.5 cm) silk beads
- ✕ 12 light Colorado topaz 4mm crystal bicones
- ✕ 18 crystal copper 8mm crystal rounds
- ✕ 18 copper 3×10mm cornflake spacers
- ✕ 6 brass 20mm African coiled rounds
- ✕ 1 gold 16mm toggle clasp
- ✕ 2 gold 2×3mm twisted crimp tubes
- ✕ 1 gold 5×16mm removable bail
- ✕ 1 antique copper 1½" (3.8 cm) square memory frame pendant
- ✕ 2 pieces of 1½" (3.8 cm) square memory glass
- ✕ 1½" (3.8 cm) square of peel-and-stick batik fabric (to fit metal frame)
- ✕ 22" (56 cm) beading wire
- ✕ Chain-nose pliers
- ✕ Wire cutter

1. Remove the paper backing from the square of fabric and attach it to 1 piece of glass. Place the second piece of glass on top of the first piece of glass and slide both pieces into the metal frame. Close frame tab.

2. Use pliers to open the bottom ring of the bail and attach it to the pendant loop.

3. Use the beading wire to string 1 crimp tube, 1 crystal bicone, and one half of the clasp. Pass back through the tube and crimp. String (1 seed bead and 1 crystal bicone) three times. String (1 cornflake spacer and 1 crystal round) three times. String (1 cornflake spacer, 1 brass round, 1 cornflake spacer, 1 crystal round, 1 silk bead, and 1 crystal round) three times. String 1 crystal bicone, 1 seed bead, and 1 crystal bicone.

4. String the bail and 1 seed bead. Repeat Step 3, reversing the stringing sequence and attaching the wire to the other half of the clasp.

Note
You can create a neutral strand necklace and make multiple framed pendants to swap out by using a removable bail on each pendant.

Color Palette

Orange

The orange color range contains some of the fiery energies of red but is gentler, with a more creative spirit. Orange is good for promoting personal power and useful for people who could use more self-esteem. I added a splash of red, smoky black, jet black, copper, yellow, and ivory to this palette.

Wild Fiber Necklace

Scrumptious fibers complement these silk beads to create a lightweight collar of colorful textures adorning your neck.

Supplies

- ✖ 1 peach 1½" (3.8 cm) jumbo silk bead
- ✖ 3 silk 2" (5 cm) beads, one each in green, gold, and bronze
- ✖ 5 silk 1" (2.5 cm) beads, one each in aqua, rust, green, teal, and gold
- ✖ 3 silk ½" (1.3 cm) beads, one each in rust, aqua, and brown
- ✖ 20 assorted 17" (43 cm) lengths of multicolored fiber strands
- ✖ 2 small rubber bands
- ✖ Scissors
- ✖ Weldbond glue

Note
You can trim the fiber edges flush with the jumbo bead or leave the edges loose as shown.

1. Lay out all the fibers next to each other.

2. Wrap a rubber band tightly around one end of the fiber bundle, making sure all the fibers are secured inside the rubber band.

3. Separate 2 or 3 strands of fiber from the bundle, use them to string the ½" (1.3 cm), 1" (2.5 cm), and 2" (5 cm) silk beads in random order, and slide the silk beads onto those fibers. (Fold a plastic bag twist tie in half and use it as a "needle" by placing the end of the 2 or 3 strands in the fold and stringing the twist tie through the beads.)

4. Straighten out fiber bundle and secure the other end with a small rubber band.

5. Shape the necklace in half as if you were wearing it and move the beads, positioning them until you are happy with their placement.

6. Slide each bead a tad, fill bead chamber with Weldbond glue and slide bead back into position hiding the glue. Repeat for all beads and let dry.

7. Use one end of the fiber bundle to string the Jumbo silk bead. Repeat with the other end of the fiber bundle, string the bead in the opposite direction.

8. Arrange the fiber ends in the jumbo silk bead so that about 1½" (3.8 cm) of fiber ends emerge from each end.

9. Fill bead chamber with glue and let dry. If necessary, trim fiber ends even.

Gallery of Jewelry Inspiration

Necklace: Two 1" (2.5 cm) fabric beads, six ½" (1.3 cm) fabric beads, tourmaline nugget, freshwater pearls, semiprecious stone chips, gold toggle clasp. Designed by Conne Gibson.

Ring: Three ¾" (2 cm) triangle fabric beads, crystal bead, crystals, silver ring blank.

Bracelet: Four ½" (1.3 cm) fabric beads, glass beads, silver beads, silver spacers, silver bangle bracelet with removable end bead.

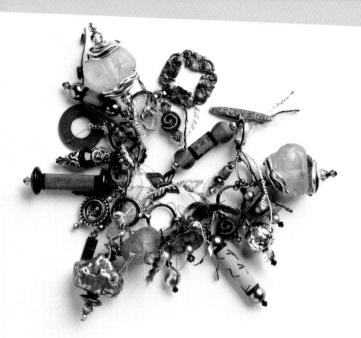

Bracelet: Two 1" (2.5 cm) fabric beads, two ½" (1.3 cm) fabric beads, resin nuggets, textured silver beads, metal charms, metal beads, glass beads, crystals, crystal pearls, bead caps, yarn, copper chain, brass toggle clasp.

Necklace: Four 1" (2.5 cm) fabric beads, two ½" (1.3 cm) fabric beads, freshwater pearls, metal charms, seed beads, crystals, silver bail, suede cord, lobster clasp.

Necklace: Three ¾" (2 cm) triangle fabric beads, four ⅜" (1 cm) triangle fabric beads, silver diamond-shaped links, crystals, detachable bail, silver chain, silver toggle clasp.

Necklace: Six ½" (1.3 cm) fabric beads with flatback embellishment, four 1" (2.5 cm) fabric beads with flatback embellishment, three 2" (5 cm) fabric beads with flatback embellishment, glass beads, crystals, resin beads, metal beads, metal charms, novelty yarn, silver neck wire.

Necklace: Four ⅝" (1.5 cm) ribbon beads, frame pendant finding, hammered copper square, detachable metal bail, crystals, crystal pearls, seed beads, copper chain, lobster clasp.

Necklace: Three 1½" (3.8 cm) wedding beads with flatback embellishment, crystals, crystal pearls, silver toggle clasp.

Necklace: Three 2" (5 cm) fabric beads with flatback embellishment, two 1" (2.5 cm) fabric beads with flatback embellishment, two ½" (1.3 cm) fabric beads with flatback embellishment, crystal pearls, suede cord, lobster clasp.

Necklace: Four ½" (1.3 cm) red leather eyelet beads, two ⅓" (1 cm) black leather eyelet beads, one ¾" (2 cm) black eyelet leather bead, textured silver beads, crystals, fine silver chain, medium silver chain, lobster clasp.

Necklace: Four 2" (5 cm) sponged fabric beads, green resin nugget, silver bead caps, silver spacers, crystals, crystal pearls, silver chain, silver toggle clasp.

Necklace: Four 1" (2.5 cm) batik fabric beads, vintage iridescent button, crystals, silver chain, pink rubber cord, lobster clasp.

Necklace: Ten ¾" (2 cm) triangle fabric beads, pewter mermaid disc pendant, small shells, fresh-water pearls, silver spacers, crystals, crystal pearls, silver toggle clasp.

Necklace: Five 1¼" (3.2 cm) triangle fabric beads, ten ½" (1.3 cm) triangle fabric beads, copper rondels, crystals, brass toggle clasp with flatback embellishment.

Necklace: Three ½" (1.3 cm) fabric beads, silver wire lace, crystals, silver chain, silver toggle clasp.

Necklace: Six ½" (1.3 cm) fabric beads, mother-of-pearl pendant with flatback embellishment, freshwater pearls, metal beads, crystals, crystal pearls, metal spacers, silver toggle clasp.

Necklace: Four 1" (2.5 cm) fabric beads, two ½" (1.3 cm) fabric beads, Venetian glass focal bead, textured silver beads, silver spacers, resin beads, crystals, seed beads, silver toggle clasp.

Techniques

Stringing

Stringing is a technique in which you use beading wire, needle and thread, or other material to gather beads into a strand.

Crimping

Crimp tubes are seamless tubes of metal that come in several sizes. To use, string a crimp tube through the connection finding. Pass back through the tube, leaving a short tail. Use the back notch of the crimping pliers to press the length of the tube down between the wires, enclosing them in separate chambers of the crescent shape. Rotate the tube 90° and use the front notch of the pliers to fold the two chambers onto themselves, forming a clean cylinder. Trim the excess wire.

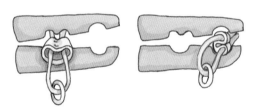

Crimp covers hide a 2mm crimp tube and give a professional finish. To attach, gently hold a crimp cover in the front notch of the crimping pliers. Insert the crimped tube and gently squeeze the pliers, encasing the tube inside the cover.

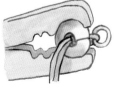 

Jump Rings

Open a jump ring by grasping each side of its opening with a pair of pliers. Don't pull apart. Instead, twist in opposite directions so that you can open and close without distorting the shape.

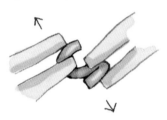

Knots

OVERHAND KNOT

The overhand knot is the basic knot for tying off thread. Make a loop with the stringing material. Pass the cord that lies behind the loop over the front cord and through the loop. Pull tight.

SQUARE KNOT

The square knot is the classic sturdy knot for securing most stringing materials. First make an overhand knot, passing the right end over the left end. Next, make another overhand knot, this time passing the left end over the right end. Pull tight.

Wireworking

SIMPLE LOOPS

To form a simple loop, use flat-nose pliers to make a 90° bend at least ½" (1.3 cm) from the end of the wire. Use round-nose pliers to grasp the wire after the bend; roll the pliers toward the bend, but not past it, to preserve the 90° bend. Use your thumb to continue the wrap around the nose of the pliers. Trim the wire next to the bend. Open a simple loop by grasping each side of its opening with a pair of pliers. Don't pull apart. Instead, twist in opposite directions so that you can open and close without distorting the shape.

WRAPPED LOOPS

To form a wrapped loop, begin with a 90° bend at least 2" (5 cm) from the end of the wire. Use round-nose pliers to form a simple loop with a tail overlapping the bend. Wrap the tail tightly down the neck of the wire to create a couple of coils. Trim the excess wire to finish. Make a double wrapped loop by wrapping the wire back up over the coils, toward the loop, and trimming at the loop. Link a wrapped loop to another loop by passing the wire through the previous loop before wrapping the neck of the new loop.

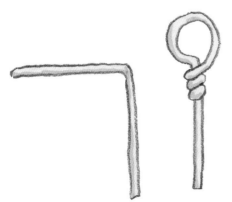

WRAPPED-LOOP BAILS

Wrapped bails turn side-drilled beads, usually teardrops, into pendants. Center the bead on a 6" (15 cm) piece of wire. Bend both ends of the wire up the sides and across the top of the bead. Bend one end straight up at the center of the bead and wrap the other wire around it to form a few coils. Form a wrapped loop with the straight-up wire, wrapping it back down over the already-formed coils. Trim the excess wire.

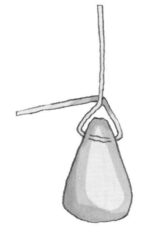

Resources

Fabric and Craft Sources

AMACO
6060 Guion Rd.
Indianapolis, IN 46254
(800) 374-1600
amaco.com
ArtEmboss copper metal sheets

Clearsnap Inc.
PO Box 98
Anacortes, WA 98221
(888) 448-4862
clearsnap.com
Molding pads (texture plates), ink pads

Devcon
30 Endicott St.
Danvers, MA 01923
(800) 626-7226
devcon.com
2 Ton and 5 Minute Epoxy (resin)

Dharma Trading Co.
1604 Fourth St.
San Rafael, CA 94901
(800) 542-5227
dharmatrading.com
Silk and dyes

Embellishment Village
15165 SW 100th Ave.
Tigard, OR 97224
(877) 639-9820
embellishmentvillage.com
Beads, yarns, Angelina fibers, Shiva Paintstiks

Grafix Arts
5800 Pennsylvania Ave.
Cleveland, OH 44137
(800) 447-2349
grafixarts.com
Stencil film, shrink plastic, Double Tack (2-sided mounting film)

Jacquard
(800) 442-0455
jacquardproducts.com
Dyes and paints

Laura Murray Designs
5021 15th Ave. South
Minneapolis, MN 554
(800) 842-4197
lauramurraydesigns.com
Shiva Paintstiks, rubbing plates, foils, adhesive, rubber stamps, texture plates

Plaid
(800) 842-4197
plaidonline.com
Decorator (texture) tools, paints, brushes, stencil cutter, stamps, stencils, blank picture pendants

Princess Mirah Design
Bali Fabrics Inc.
21787 Eighth St. East
Ste. #1
Sonoma, CA 95476
princessmirah.com
Batik fabrics, peel and stick batiks

Ranger Industries
15 Park Rd.
Tinton Falls, NJ 07724
(732) 389-3535
rangerink.com
Adirondack Color Wash (spray dye), embossing pads and powders, memory frames, flexible Teflon sheets, Beadazzles (mini beads), pigment powders

Sherrill Kahn
17116 Escalon Dr.
Encino, CA 91436
(818) 788-6730
impressmenow.com
Rubber stamps and books

Silk Connection
PO Box 425
Healdsburg, CA 95448
(800) 442-0455
silkconnection.com
Silk

Staedtler
21900 Plummer St.
Chatsworth, CA 91311
(818) 882-6000
staedtler.us
Carving tools

Martha Stewart
marthastewartcrafts.com
Ribbons, stamps

Tandy Leather Factory
3847 East Loop 820 South
Fort Worth, TX 76119
(800) 433-3201
tandyleatherfactory.com
Leather

Tsukineko
17640 NE 65th St.
Redmond, WA 98052
(425) 883-7733
tsukineko.com
StazOn permanent ink

Weldbond
225 Cash St.
Jacksonville, TX 75766
(800) 388-2001
weldbondusa.com
Glue

Beads and Jewelry Sources

Absolute Crystal Components
3810 Oceanic Dr., Ste. 205
Oceanside, CA 92056
(800) 758-2960
absolutecrystalcomponents.com
Swarovski crystals, pearls, flatbacks, jewelry findings, shell beads

Alacarte Clasps
PO Box 977
Forestville, CA 95436
(800) 977-2825
alacarteclasps.com
Wire lace, removable bails, glue-in post earrings and crystals, beads

Artbeads.com
11901 137th Ave. Ct. KPN
Gig Harbor, WA 98329
(866) 715-BEAD (2323)
artbeads.com
Swarovski crystals, various beads, wood bead frames

Artistic Wire Ltd.
752 North Larch Ave.
Elmhurst, IL 60126
(630) 530-7567
artisticwire.com
Craft wire

Beadalon
440 Highlands Blvd.
Coatesville, PA 19320
(866) 4BEADALON
(423-2325)
beadalon.com
Beading wire, beads, hot-fix tool, heat-set flatback crystals, crimps, chain, tools

The Bead Goes On
PO Box 592
14 Church St.
Vineyard Haven
Martha's Vineyard, MA 02568
(508) 693-7618
beadgoeson.com
Resin nuggets

Beads and Pieces
1320 Commerce St., Ste. C
Petaluma, CA 94954
(707) 765-2890
beadsandpieces.com
Resin beads

Beyond Beadery
PO Box 460
Rollinsville, CO 80474
(800) 840-5548
beyondbeadery.com
Seed beads, Swarovski crystals

Creativity Inc.
7855 Hayvenhurst Ave.
Van Nuys, CA 91406
(800) 377-6705
creativityinc.com
Beads, findings, chain

Darice
13000 Darice Pkwy.
Park 82
Strongsville, OH 44149
(800) 321-1494
darice.com
Findings, beads

Fusion Beads
13024 Stone Ave. N
Seattle, WA 98133
(206) 781-9512
fusionbeads.com
*Swarovski crystals, beads,
   charms, findings*

Gita Maria
PO Box 918
Gold Beach, OR 97444
(877) 247-9647
gitamaria.com
Enamel pendants

Green Girl Studios
PO Box 19389
Asheville, NC 28815
(828) 298-2263
greengirlstudios.com
*Handcrafted pewter and
   sterling beads*

Ilene Combs Blanco
Bama Beads
603 Pratt Ave.
Huntsville, AL 35801
(256) 534-6010
bamabeads.com
White turquoise

JewelrySupply.com
301 Derek Pl.
Roseville, CA 95678
(866) 503-1150
jewelrysupply.com
*Swarovski crystals, charms,
   flatbacks, findings*

Kristal Wick Creations
(866) 811-1376
KristalWick.com
*Sassy Silkies, ceramic
   kitty-mermaid beads,
   shell pendants*

Lady from Venice
theladyfromvenice.com
Venetian glass beads

Lillypilly Designs
PO Box 270136
Louisville, CO 80027
(303) 543-8673
lillypillydesigns.com
Etched shell pendants

Mykonos
245 Main St.
Hyannis, MA 02601
(888) 695-6667
mykonosbeads.com
Metal beads

Natural Touch
PO Box 2713
Petaluma, CA 94953
(707) 781-0808
naturaltouchbeads.com
Resin beads

Paula Radke
PO Box 1088
Morro Bay, CA 93443
(805) 772-5451
paularadke.com
Dichroic glass beads

Rings & Things
PO Box 450
Spokane, WA 99210-0450
(800) 366-2156
rings-things.com
Findings, charms, chain

Soft Flex Company
PO Box 80
Sonoma, CA 95476
(866) 925-3539
softflexcompany.com
Beading wire

Somerset Silver
PO Box 253
Mukilteo, WA 98275
(425) 641-3666
somerset-silver.com
Silver beads, findings, pendants

**Swarovski DIY (Do It
Yourself) Division**
One Kenney Dr.
Cranston, RI 02920
(401) 463-6400
create-your-style.com
*Crystals, pearls, flatbacks,
   online design tool*

TierraCast
3177 Guerneville Rd.
Santa Rosa, CA 95401
(800) 222-9939
tierracast.com
Beads, findings, toggles

Two Cranes
PO Box 83
Magdalena, NM 87825
(575) 571-1760
2cranes.biz
Natural stone beads

Via Murano
17654 Newhope St.
Ste. A
Fountain Valley, CA 92708
(877) 842-6872
viamurano.com
*Twisted Tornado crimps,
   Snapeez jump rings*

Vintaj
PO Box 256
Galena, IL 61036
vintaj.com
Brass findings, toggles, beads

Bibliography

Bautista, Traci. *Collage Unleashed*. Cincinnati, Ohio: North Light Books, 2006.

Creative Publishing International. *Exploring Textile Arts: The Ultimate Guide to Manipulating, Coloring, and Embellishing Fabrics*. Chanhassen, Minnesota: Creative Publishing International, 2002.

Deighan, Helen. *Dyeing in Plastic Bags: No Mess No Fuss Just Great Colours!* Grayshott, Hampshire, United Kingdom: Crossways Patch, 2001.

Kahn, Sherrill. *Creating with Paint: New Ways, New Materials*. Woodville, Washington: Martingale & Company, 2001.

———. *Creative Embellishments: For Paper, Jewelry, Fabric and More*. Woodville, Washington: Martingale & Company, 2007.

———. *Creative Stamping with Mixed Media Techniques*. Cincinnati, Ohio: North Light Books, 2003.

McGraw, MaryJo. *Creative Rubber Stamping Techniques*. Cincinnati, Ohio: North Light Books, 1998.

Stokes, Shelly. *Paintstiks on Fabric: Simple Techniques, Fantastic Results*. Miltona, Minnesota: Cedar Canyon Textiles, 2005.

Index

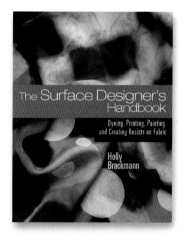
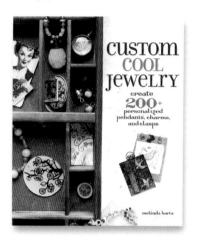
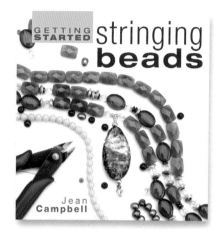